PSYCHIC CONFLICT IN SPANISH AMERICA

Six Essays on the Psychohistory of the Region

Marvin Goldwert, Ph.D.

Professor of History
New York Institute of Technology

UNIVERSITY
PRESS OF
AMERICA

Copyright © 1982 by
University Press of America, Inc.
P.O. Box 19101, Washington, D.C. 20036

Printed in the United States of America

Library of Congress Cataloging in Publication Data

Goldwert, Marvin.
Psychic conflict in Spanish America.

Contents: The conquest of Mexico as Kairos -- The
search for the lost father-figure in Spanish American
history -- Rebellion, alienation, and conformity in
the lives of the caudillos -- [etc.]
1. Latin America--History--Psychological aspects--
Addresses, essays, lectures. 2. Psychohistory--
Addresses, essays, lectures. I. Title.
F1410.G655   980'.001'9   82-45059
ISBN 0-8191-2413-3   AACR2
ISBN 0-8191-2414-1 (pbk.)

To my students at the New York Institute of Technology

Acknowledgements

The six essays which comprise this volume represent over a decade and a half of my quest to understand the Spanish American psyche. First published in 1966, the fifth of these essays, "Dichotomies of Militarism in Argentina," sparked my interest in psychic conflict in Spanish America. In groping for a unifying idea to explain Argentine militarism, I was led to a theory of conflict between traditional and modern values within the military mind. After incorporating this thesis into a volume on Argentine militarism, published by The University of Texas Press in 1972 under the title, <u>Democracy, Militarism, and Nationalism in Argentina, 1930-1966: An Interpretation</u>, I entered upon the formal study of psychoanalysis as a special student in the Psychoanalytic Center, New York City. From this cross-fertilization of historical and psychoanalytic disciplines has flowed a book, <u>History as Neurosis: Paternalism and Machismo in Spanish America</u> (University Press of America, 1980), and the five other essays contained in this volume. Taken together, they are a record of my personal sojourn into the mind of Spanish America.

In this personal quest, I have been inspired by four of my former Professors of Latin American history: Harry Bernstein (Brooklyn College); Lewis Hanke and Thomas F. McGann (The University of Texas); and, Arthur P. Whitaker (University of Pennsylvania, deceased). My students at the New York Institute of Technology have always been a source of delight and stimulation for my scholarly endeavors. Sympathetic colleagues at the New York Institute of Technology, such as Sam P. Pinkerton, Ahmed A. Majid, and K. Chandrasekar, have provided continual encouragement. Finally, my parents, Aaron (deceased) and Frieda Goldwert, have provided the spiritual support without which my scholarly work could not have moved forward.

Marvin Goldwert

Table of Contents

Introduction

Psychic conflict is at the core of Freudian thought. According to Philip Rieff, Freud was concerned with "the 'civil war' which is neurosis...a civil war within the mind."[1] In the six essays which follow, three of which use Freud as a point-of-departure, psychic conflict is examined in Spanish American history. For Spanish America was born, reared, and nurtured in psychic conflicts which reverberate down to this day.

One of the aims of the following essays is to offer an alternative sense of time and framework for Spanish America's conflicted history. True to Freudian thought, time is viewed as <u>Kairos</u> in the first two essays. By Kairos, I mean trauma time and the pregnant moment, those crucial early happenings in a civilization's history which overtake all ensuing developments. Kairos is qualitative over quantitative time, emotional over chronological time, and psychological over historical time. Just as in the life-history of individuals early trauma shapes their entire existence, so, too, in the life-history of civilizations Kairos (traumatic event) is the crucial force in determining their development. Kairos determines history, for it lives in the mass unconscious, sometimes latent as tradition and sometimes manifest as in the cyclical return-of-the-repressed, but always shaping man's destiny. In the first two essays, I trace the pathology of Spanish America to two kairotic events--the Conquest of Mexico in the sixteenth century and the overthrow of Spanish kingship in the years 1808 to 1826. Each of these traumatic events have triggered conflictual behavior-patterns in Spanish America which have endured down to this day.

If Kairos is the sense of time in Freudian historical thought, history-as-neurosis is the cyclical framework. As the first two essays point out, Freud believed that the stages of neurosis in the individual unfold as the collective stages of history. Psychic conflicts born in Kairos (trauma time) are followed by "childhood neurosis," which is followed by "latency," and which, in turn, is followed by the "return-of-the-repressed." Each of the two kairotic events--the Conquest and the overthrow of Kingship--triggered related "neurotic" cycles in Spanish American history.

Òut of Kairos and history-as-neurosis, there emerged the three conflicted historical figures which are treated in the three essays which follow: the caudillo, the _macho_, and the military man. In essay III, the nineteenth-century caudillo is viewed as an uprooted social "misfit," who, having broken with family, social group, or formal education, yearned for the power and prestige of political authority. In overcoming his sense of social uprootedness, the caudillo strove for identification with the creole oligarchy. The creole oligarchy, in turn, was quite prepared to rule through these social "misfits" in the turbulent "childhood neurosis" of Spanish American history (1826-1870s).

More enduring than even the caudillo in Spanish American life is the social type known as the _macho_ (virile he-man). Heir to both the conquistador and the caudillo, the Mexican _macho_ is viewed in essay IV as fleeing from femininity into death. A convergence of historical and contemporary conditioning is seen in the causation of the conflicted Mexican _macho's_ flight from femininity into death.

In essay V, I treat the psychic conflicts of Argentina's army officers, of those military men who represent the "return-of-the-repressed" in the "neurotic" cycle. The Argentine army officer, motivated by corporate rather than social interests, is viewed as caught in an insoluble conflict between traditional and modern values. On the one hand, he desires social order, traditionalism, Catholicism, and simple historic patriotism. On the other, he longs for technical modernization and heavy industry to bolster the military machine. But modernization and industrialization erode traditional values and challenge social order by ushering in a complex society. How to reconcile his traditional values with the requirements of technical modernization, has been, I argue, the fundamental dilemma of military men not only in Argentina, but throughout Spanish America.

Finally, in essay VI, I deal with the failure of the Spanish American middle class to lift the weight of Kairos by making social democracy a reality on that continent. Here, too, psychic conflict is paramount. A quote from Victor Alba illustrates such conflict as he describes the "schizophrenia" of the middle class-- "either it must arouse the submerged masses in order, with them, to destroy the power of the oligarchy and create a capitalist society; or it must make an effort, from within the oligarchic society, to win control of the government." Fearful of the masses, the Spanish American middle class has chosen the latter course. In terms of the social revolution, the middle class faces a dilemma described by anthropologist Charles Wagley: "The middle class of Latin America helps to create the pre-conditions for revolution, but it really does not want to live it through. To provide the same conditions of life for the mass of the people which the middle class itself enjoys might well destroy its own favored conditions." Hence, the middle class, once the harbinger of great hope for Spanish America, has failed to lift the weight of Kairos from the continent. Once again, psychic conflict proves as important as socio-economic conflict in determining the destiny of Spanish America.

NOTE

[1]Philip Rieff, <u>Freud: The Mind of the Moralist</u> (3rd ed., Chicago: University of Chicago Press, 1979), p. 63.

I

The Conquest of Mexico as Kairos:
A Freudian View

In a trailblazing article on "The Meaning of
History and Religion in Freud's Thought," Philip Rieff
declared: "Freud was fascinated and horrified by the
power of the past....For Freud, a given life history,
even as a given group history, must be examined in
terms of the experience of crucial events occurring
necessarily at a specific historical time. What is
crucial needs have happened early. There had to be a
Kairos, that crucial time in the past that is decisive
for what then must come after. Kairos may be thought
of as antinomical to Chronos, mathematical time in
which each unit is qualitatively identical. Kairotic
time, on the other hand, is not qualitatively identi-
cal--rather the reverse. Thus, for Freud, memory time
is always kairotic. For example, the kairotic time of
childhood may overwhelm vast stretches of later chronological time. This identifies Kairos with traumatic
event..."[1]

Let no historian confuse Freud's Kairos with his
own mild, open-ended concept of turning-points. For
Freud's "cyclical, organic model of Kairos" differs
fundamentally from the "unilinear, time-directed model"
of the traditional historian. "Reducing change to constancy, Freud collapses history into nature, religion
and politics into psychology."[2] Kairos determines history, for it lives in the mass unconscious, sometimes
latent as tradition and sometimes manifest as in the
cyclical return-of-the-repressed, but always shaping
man's destiny. A knowledge of Kairos indicates that
history holds few surprises.

In attempting to fuse historical man with psychological man, Freud envisioned a psychohistory set
within a framework of history-as-neurosis. Although
fully developed in Moses and Monotheism, the seeds of
this framework had been planted in his previous historical works. He had long contended that the psychic
processes of the individual unfold in the collective
societies of history. Psychic states work themselves
out as the stages of history, for social psychology is
merely the reflection of changes in the individual's
mind. The stages of neurosis in the individual are
the stages of the collective history of societies.

1

Freud's historical formula reads as follows: "early trauma-defense (childhood neurosis)--latency--outbreak of the neurosis--partial return of the re-pressed material."[3] In formulating history-as-neurosis, Freud instructed us to look to early trauma (Kairos) as the determining forces in the history of a society. Like neurosis in the individual, the aetiology of social illness is to be traced to early experiences. Early trauma brings early symptoms known as "defense," or "childhood neurosis," which are associated with the early life of society. "Childhood neurosis" is gener-ally followed by a period of undisturbed development known as "latency." Bouyed by increasing maturity, the society takes up the battle against neurosis. Although some sort of stability is established, this is more apparent than real. For, at puberty or later, soci-eties, like neurotic individuals, begin to feel the afflictions of the past (Kairos) which return to haunt them. Full-blown neurosis erupts as the maturing soci-iety experiences the "return-of-the-repressed."

That Freud tied this model of time and cyclical change to a mythical primeval murder, probably explains why few historians have taken his approach seriously. Yet, detached from primal parricide, Kairos has much to recommend it to the historian. Who will deny that in certain traumatic events, such as the Spanish Conquest of Mexico, one can sense the Kairos which decisively shaped the living history of Spanish America? Radiat-ing from this central event were the psychic tremors which still shake the collective unconscious of that region. It is the purpose of this paper to analyze the Spanish Conquest of Mexico, that traumatic first rape of an advanced Indian civilization, as Kairos, to treat it as the determining and ever-recurring trauma which shaped all of Spanish American history.

Viewed as Kairos, the Conquest must be stripped of romance in order to ascertain the recurrent behavior-patterns it injected into the stream of Spanish Ameri-can history. In the analysis which follows, four such behavior-patterns are discerned: 1) God and Man: Religion and Power; 2) Male and Female: "Metaphysical Bisexuality"; 3) Man and Government: Rebellion and Order; and, 4) Leader and Follower: The Tradition of Charismatic Leadership.

1. God and Man: Religion and Power

R. C. Padden, who spent many years studying the

Conquest of Mexico, concluded: "Central to this problem was the fact that in both Spanish and Indian minds sovereignty was inextricably associated with religion."[4] Religion and power have ever since been associated in the Spanish American mind. From the Freudian standpoint, the relationship between Catholicism and power may be analyzed from three vantage-points: first, the introduction in kairotic time of a tradition of humanitarian reformism in the Church which did battle with the more conservative defenders of the faith; second, the relationship of these contending forces to the Freudian conception of God in the Catholic religion; and, third, the fate of the humanitarian-conservative dichotomy as it traversed the cycle of history-as-neurosis.

With regard to the first vantage-point, Lewis Hanke reminds us that "the Spanish conquest of America was far more than a remarkable military and political exploit; that it was also one of the greatest attempts the world had seen to make Christian precepts prevail in the relations between peoples. This attempt became basically a spirited defense of the rights of the Indians, which rested on two of the most fundamental assumptions a Christian can make: namely that all men are equal before God, and that a Christian has responsibility for the welfare of his brothers no matter how alien or lowly they may be."[5] Hence, introduced in kairotic time was a humanitarian concern for social justice which emanated mainly from members of the clergy like Bartolomé de Las Casas. It is the fate of this humanitarian reformism which must concern us in this Freudian analysis.

From Ernest Gruening, we learn that after this "most luminous page in the story of the Spanish Conquest of America, the zeal for conversion flagged and priests of a different mold replaced the pioneers... the luxury and magnificence of the clergy grew apace... The asceticism of the pioneers was forgotten. A new spirit of arrogant debauchery infected the ruling minority..."[6] The humanitarian-reformist tradition, the kairotic counterpoise to the rapist-conquistador, was thus driven into the spiritual unconscious.

Granted that a humanitarian-religious tradition was implanted in kairotic time, the question is: What can the Freudian approach contribute toward explaining the tortuous association of religion and power in ensuing Spanish American history? Freud believed that

3

man projects his psychic conflicts, especially the Oedipal, into his conceptions of God. In writing of Christianity in Moses and Monotheism, Freud concluded: "Its main doctrine, to be sure, was the reconciliation with God the Father, the expiation of the crime committed against Him; but the other side of the relationship manifested itself in the Son, who had taken the guilt on His shoulders, becoming God Himself beside the Father and in truth in place of the Father. Originally a Father religion, Christianity became a Son religion. The fate of having to displace the Father it could not escape."[7] In accordance with Freud's observation, how could the Father-Son rivalry, inherent in the psychodynamics of Christianity, become associated with power in Spanish America?

It may be argued that ever since Kairos, the Spanish Americans have unconsciously acted out the great psychic-political conflict of religious history. The humanitarians may be viewed as the upstart proponents of the compassionate Son-religion; the conservatives as the stern, established defenders of Father-authority. For the imposition of Christianity upon Spanish America, created a trinity of spiritual allegiance--God (the Father), the Son-God, and the Virgin Mary. Women and the eclectic Indians, the submerged, opted for the Virgin Mary and in their submissiveness sought a benign mother-figure. On the other hand, creole and mestizo males unconsciously followed divine models in their struggles for power, playing out the larger Oedipal theme of compassionate Son-God versus stern Father-God.

And this conflict, forged in Kairos, continues into the present. Today, once again, rebellious Catholic priests are turning to the compassionate Son-God religion in their challenge of stern Father-authority. How Spanish Americans have reached the point where again the question of God and man, religion and power, central to the Conquest, has moved to the center of Spanish American history, belongs to the cyclical framework of history-as-neurosis.

As has been shown, a humanitarian-religious impulse in the Conquest was soon smothered in the aftermath of that historical period. This humanitarian impulse, lodged in the lower clergy, reappeared briefly at the beginning of "childhood neurosis" (1808-1910) in the wars of independence (1808-1826). It was then that the lower clergy, the poorer members of the hierarchy, disobeyed their bishops and identified themselves with the independence movement. Despite their allegiance to the liberating movements, the clergy soon found themselves embroiled in the church-state struggle which followed the attainment of independence. In the neurotic conflict of national childhood, "the quarrel between the anticlerical lawyer, steeped in concepts of absolute sovereignty, and the priest, who looked upon all matters that might touch the soul and affect human salvation as the special responsibility of the Church, ended in a conflict that was often bitter and bloody. The lawyer won the battle."[8]

After a hundred years of conflict, the bitterness was gradually "attenuated"[9] so that, during "latency" (1917-1940s), the Church returned to its passive conservative stance. The proponents of the conservative Father-God religion have, however, been challenged anew since the aftermath of World War II. First, the proponents of the compassionate Son-God humanitarianism voiced the social duties expressed in the Rerum Novarum of Pope Leo XIII. In recent years, this mild form of Christian Democracy is being eclipsed by a more militant "liberation" movement within the Church. Hence, once again, the great psychic-political-religious conflict, rooted in Kairos, has emerged as "the return-of-the-repressed."

2. Male and Female: "Metaphysical Bisexuality"

The concept of "metaphysical bisexuality" is borrowed from sociologist Salvador Reyes Nevares, who views it as the psychohistorical basis of machismo.[10] I shall expand Reyes Nevares' concept by making Cortés and Montezuma the popular psychological personifications of this haunting historical condition. In Conquest, Cortés, the first macho, played the role of aggressive Spanish-masculine rapist and Montezuma that of passive Indian-feminine victim, a betrayal of the great Aztec military tradition.

This polarity was recognized by the great nineteenth-century historian William H. Prescott. When in 1520, the captive Montezuma lies to his people by cowardly declaring "I am no prisoner" of the Spaniards, he is met with derision by the Aztec crowd. "Base Aztec," Prescott makes them exclaim, "woman, coward, the white men have made you a woman--fit only to weave and spin."[11] In assessing Montezuma's role in relation to the Spaniards, Prescott agreed with their judgment: "He at once conceded all that they demanded --his treasures, his power, even his person. For their sake, he forsook his wonted occupations, his pleasures, his most familiar habits. He might be said to forego his nature; and, as his subjects asserted, to change his sex and become a woman."[12]

Indigenous America thus, at first, had no native masculine father-defender. Nor, on the other hand, did it have a universal mother it could be proud of. Of Mexico's universal mother, the Malinche, Cortés' Indian mistress and interpreter, Victor Alba has written that Mexicans of today look upon her "much as the French and the Dutch regarded the village girls who fraternized with Germans during World War II. Anyone who adopts a position not strictly nationalistic is labeled a "Malinchist" and lumped with those who can see some merit in foreign things or who appreciate the foreign more than the Mexican. This type of snobbery abounds and is branded with the abhorred name of the Indian princess."[13] In accordance with this spirit, recent commentators like Octavio Paz and Salvador Reyes Nevares have labeled the Malinche "as the symbol of surrender," and have declared that she plays a "traumatic role" in the psychology of the Mexican as the personification of female-Indian collaboration with the hated Spaniard.[14]

Fear of femininity and of female betrayal, forged in Kairos, are the twin psychic insecurities at the core of Spanish American machismo. Haunted by the femininity of the Indian father, the mestizo seeks to assert his Hispanic masculinity through the conquest of women in all quarters. Haunted by this "metaphysical bisexuality," the mestizo veers between Spanish-aggressor and Indian-supplicant, a polarity which buttresses the sense of hierarchy in Spanish America. Rooted, in part, in "metaphysical bisexuality," is the dominance-passivity syndrome which underpins the historic relationships between patrón and client, caudillo and masses, president and party follower, revolutionary leader and faction, army officer and civilian populace.

Unconsciously, mestizo societies of Spanish America still seek revenge for female betrayal. In the collective unconscious, women are still equated with the Indian element of mestizaje. The Mexican psychoanalyst, Santiago Ramírez, recognized this when he declared: "Woman is devalued to the extent to which she is identified with the native; man is elevated in

virtue of his identification with the conqueror and
master. Though also known elsewhere, this equipara-
tion of masculinity with aggression, and of femininity
with passivity, assumes in our civilization its most
striking and dramatic forms."15 Male insecurity and
female subordination, both of these have their roots
in the Conquest as Kairos.

Having treated "metaphysical bisexuality" as a
socially dynamic concept, it remains for me to place
it within the context of history-as-neurosis. As an
act of rape, the Conquest of Mexico sent tremors
throughout Spanish American history. During "childhood
neurosis" (1808-1870s), after the original trauma incu-
bated in the body politic, the caudillo, successor to
the macho-conquistador, used charismatic manliness to
impose himself on the passive-feminine masses. After
a period of "latency" (1870s-1910), Mexico and Spanish
America witnessed two bursts of rampant machismo which
shattered temporary peace. In Mexico, the deceptive
"latency" established by Porfirio Díaz was broken by a
new revolutionary machismo which spread havoc in the
land. In the rest of Spanish America, the year 1930,
Depression-time, witnessed the arrival of modern militarism on the scene, a phenomenon which represents the
"return-of-the-repressed" in the history of the region.
In part, an institutionalized return to machismo,
modern militarism pitted the laconic, military man-of-
action, heir to conquistador and caudillo, against the
"babbling," effete professional politicians. In modern
militarism, the machista cycle of history-as-neurosis
is closed.

3. Man and Government: Rebellion and Order

In treating theme III, I shall again do so in
terms of psychic conflicts born in Kairos. I use as my
point-of-departure a stimulating statement by J. H.
Parry: "The rule of the conquistadores was quarrelsome
and brief. They had gone to America at their own ex-
pense, endured great hardships, risked their lives and
(such as they were) their fortunes, without much prac-
tical help from the government at home; and the government never fully trusted them. Most of the leaders
died violent deaths. Among those who survived the
hardships, the campaigns and the knives of jealous
rivals, very few were entrusted with administrative
power. Obviously they were not men of a kind likely to
settle down as obedient bureaucrats; and it was natural
that the Crown should supplant them--once their

7

conquests were secure--with men of its choice: offi-
cials, lawyers, ecclesiastics. Their followers and
successors, however--the second and third ranks of the
conquest, a wave of emigration representative of almost
every class and group in Spain, except the highest
nobility--settled in considerable numbers in the lands
they had conquered, and created their own characteristic society, highly resistant to bureaucratic regula-
tion. This society--turbulent, aristocratic, loosely
organized and jealous--was to set an enduring stamp
upon the whole story of Spanish America."16

Implicit in Parry's statement is a theme of history-as-neurosis and the constant impact of Kairos
(i.e., "enduring stamp"). Introduced by the trauma of
Conquest was an enduring and recurring conflict between
action and law, charisma and bureaucracy, and rebellion
and obedience. In this respect, it is well to remember
that the Spanish Conquest of Mexico was executed by a
charismatic man-of-action in defiance of legal authority. Had not Cortés rebelled against the authorities
of Cuba? Was not the foundation of Vera Cruz in Mexico
a ploy to endow Cortés and his expedition with post-
rebellion legal authority? As John E. Fagg so color-
fully points out, until 1523, when the king finally
consented to legalize Cortés' position, "the great conquistador was an outlaw leader of a gang of fili-
busters."17

Born in kairotic time, this tension between rebellion and obedience is a constancy which can be inter-
preted within the framework of history-as-neurosis..
Conquest was a time of rebellion over obedience, charisma over bureaucracy, action over law. This tension
lurked beneath the surface of colonial stability. It
found expression during the "childhood neurosis" of
Spanish America (1826-1870s), when, after the overthrow
of royal paternalism, pandemonium broke loose in the
form of caudillismo. Were not the caudillos charismatic men-of-action, who, like Cortés, first rebelled
against legal authority and later formulated constitutions to sanction their acts? At the risk of repeti-
tion, let me repeat the continuous and cyclical nature
of Spanish American history. After mad caudillismo
came "latency" (1870s-WW I), when legal authority and
temporary stability were established by the father-
presidents who integrated their societies into the
world economy. But legality and growing complexity did
not mean maturity, for between World War I and the
Great Depression, the men-of-action rose in defiance of

law, authority, bureaucracy, and obedience. In the Mexican Revolution (1910-1917), charismatic revolutionaries, heirs to the conquerors and caudillos, again spread havoc in the land in the historic "return-of-the-repressed." As has been stated, in Spanish America, after "latency" foundered on the Great Depression (1929-1930), the military came charging into the historical arena to close the cycle of history-as-neurosis.

4. Leader and Follower:
The Tradition of Charismatic Leadership

If Cortés was the first rebel, he was also the first charismatic leader in Spanish American history. In this respect, let me permit a Spaniard, Salvador de Madariaga, to reflect the elements of charisma implanted by Cortés in kairotic time. Madariaga has much to say about Cortés' leadership, and his conclusions are generally favorable. I have selected two of Madariaga's comments as noteworthy. After Cortés founds Vera Cruz and Montezuma's messengers arrive, Madariaga declares: "So fate, after all, was playing into Cortés' hands--as it always does into the hands of the strong."[18] After Cortés personally destroys the Indian idols, Madariaga declares: "His action was not below reason, but above reason. And that is why it is legendary, as are all those actions whereby man rises above men."[19]

These were some of the attributes of a charismatic leader whom Prescott declares "was, in truth, the very mirror of the times in which he lived."[20] In Madariaga's statements, we have the kairotic essense of Hispanic charisma--fate, strength, personalism, machismo, irrationality, and action; all, apart from law and obedience, by which "man rises above men." That the Hispanic tradition of charistmatic leadership and personalism may be traced back to Cortés and the Conquest, is indubitable.

Conclusion

Arguing that Spanish America has never "assimilated" its past, Leopolda Zea declares: "The contradiction between conqueror and the conquered was still not resolved when we decided to become republicans, liberals, and democrats according to the model which great modern countries, especially Anglo-Saxon ones, gave us."[21] The Freudian time-model of Kairos holds that this contradiction has still not, indeed probably never will be, completely resolved.

The Spanish Conquest of Mexico was the first violent overthrow of an advanced native civilization, and
thus merits our attention as the kairotic event for all
of Spanish American history. It injected into the
stream of Spanish American history many of the current
political behavior-patterns: the different politico-
religious attitudes toward society; dominant male-
female relationships; political man's stance towards
authority; and, the quintessence of charisma. As a
violent act of rape, the Conquest of Mexico was certain
to leave an indelible stamp on all of Spanish American
history.

Governments in Spanish America may rise and fall,
societies and economies may change, but the psychic
conflicts of the region, forged in Kairos, remain
largely constant. Chained to the wheel of kairotic
time, Spanish Americans will continue to project their
Oedipal conflicts into the role of Christianity in
political life. Indeed, perhaps the only current hope
for Spanish America lies today in the Church, or elements thereof which are trying to alter the relationship between God and man. Haunted by "metaphysical
bisexuality," some of the Spanish American nations will
continue to veer between charismatic he-man and passive
"feminine" masses. Others, caught in the tide of
history-as-neurosis, will never escape the conflict between action and law, rebellion and obedience, and personality and institutions.

Notes

1. Philip Rieff, "The Meaning of History and Religion in Freud's Thought" in Bruce Mazlish, ed., Psychoanalysis and History (New York: Grosset and Dunlap, 1971), pp. 25-26.

2. Ibid., pp. 26-27.

3. Sigmund Freud, Moses and Monotheism, Trans. Katherine Jones (New York: Vintage Books, 1967), pp. 90-91.

4. R. C. Padden, The Hummingbird and the Hawk: Conquest and Sovereignty in the Valley of Mexico, 1503-1541 (Ohio State University Press, 1967), p. viii.

5. Lewis Hanke, The Spanish Struggle for Justice in the Conquest of America (Boston: Little, Brown, and Co., 1965), p. 1.

6. Ernest Gruening, Mexico and Its Heritage (New York: Appleton-Century-Crofts, 1928), pp. 173-175.

7. Freud, Moses and Monotheism, p. 175.

8. Frank Tannenbaum, Ten Keys to Latin America (New York: Vintage Books, 1966), p. 62.

9. Ibid.

10. Santiago Reyes Nevares, "El machismo en México," Mundo Nuevo, no. 46 (April 1970), pp. 14-19.

11. William H. Prescott, History of the Conquest of Mexico and History of the Conquest of Peru (New York: The Modern Library, ?), pp. 421-422.

12. Ibid., pp. 437-438.

13. Victor Alba, The Mexicans: The Making of a Nation (New York: Praeger, 1967), p. 13

14. Reyes Nevares, "El machismo en Mexico," pp. 16-17.

15. Quoted in Stanislav Andreski, Parasitism and Subversion: The Case of Latin America (New York: Schocken Books, 1966), p. 53.

16. J. H. Parry, The Spanish Seaborne Empire (New York: Knopf, 1966), p. 98.

17. John Edwin Fagg, Latin America: A General History (2nd ed., New York: Macmillan, 1969), p. 92.

18. Salvador de Madariaga, Hernán Cortés, Conqueror of Mexico (Coral Gables: University of Miami Press, 1942), p. 139.

19. Ibid., p. 293.

20. Prescott, History of the Conquest of Mexico, p. 149.

21. Leopoldo Zea, The Latin-American Mind, Trans. James H. Abbott and Lowell Dunham (Norman: University of Oklahoma Press, 1963), p. 6.

II

The Search for the Lost Father-Figure in Spanish American History:
A Freudian View*

Sigmund Freud was more than the father of psychoanalysis; he was also one of the great classical philosophers of history.[1] In Freud's historical thought, we have the framework for an analysis of the past which parallels the formation of neuroses in the life history of the individual.[2] Like psychological man, historical man is the victim of events (trauma) from the past. Etched on the brain of historical man, are memories which endure through time, become part of the "archaic heritage," and are transmitted from one generation to another. Then, like the "return of the repressed" in neurotic individuals, societies feel the afflictions of the past, which return to haunt them. That Freud stressed the killing of the primeval father by his jealous sons, an event of dubious historical veracity, should not obscure the value of his historical framework. In Freudian thought, the psychic stages of the individual unfold in the collective societies of history.[3]

During the colonial period of Spanish American history, the paternal rule of the King was in harmony with the structure of the patrilineal family, the basic unit of society. The patrilineal family had its roots in Imperial Spain. In that country the father was the unquestioned ruler of the family circle, and this deep-rooted tradition was transferred by the colonists to the New World. During the colonial period, King and Church served as sources of patriarchal control, fortifying the prevailing structure of the family. God, King, and the Father were the paternal triarchy of colonial Spanish American society.

In a recent book, Richard Graham has analyzed with striking perception the role played by the Spanish King as the father of Spanish American society:[4]

---

*Reprinted from The Americas, Volume XXXIV, April 1978, Number 4, pp. 532-536.

The Hapsburgs thought of themselves
as patriarchs who occupied their
position, not because of the divine
right of kings, but because of the
divine right of fathers. According
to the Hapsburg view, God had or-
dained the family as the basic unit
of society, and the family was hier-
archically structured with the
father as its head; therefore the
king was also the head of a simi-
larly structured family with every
member of society occupying a place
within it that was fixed by God.
In a sense, the Hapsburgs ruled over
a family not a state. . . . No
legislation could change the deeply
meaningful link between king and
subject, just as no law could alter
the biological connection between
father and son. The Bourbons thought
somewhat differently about the relationship between king and subject
. . . the Bourbons were more apt to
think of the king as a ruler than as
a father and to judge him by the
efficiency of his rule rather than
by his love for his subjects. The
Spanish-Americans clung to the Hapsburg image of the patriarchal state
and resisted the Bourbons' political
philosophy.

But the beloved royal father-figure had favorite
"sons." Sibling rivalry is as old as the family. In
Freudian thought, male children have ambivalent feelings toward the father, rooted of course in the Oedipal conflict. Social groups may share such thoughts,
although the origins of the conflict need not be sexual. In colonial Spanish America, ambivalence towards
the royal father-figure was magnified by criollo
jealousy of the favored peninsulares. The peninsulares, Spaniards born in Spain, were given control of
the highest offices in the land. This, of course,
created a discontented group of "children," the
criollos, white Spaniards born in America, who were
largely excluded from power.

In the years 1808 to 1825, the criollos led the
way in overthrowing the royal father-figure. This was

14

the central and "traumatic" event in all Spanish American history. It represented the acting out of Oedipal desires to slay the father, creating a collective guilt which Spanish America has never overcome. Much of the rebelliousness in modern Spanish American history represents a search for a paternal replacement for the Kings of Spain. The presence of personalism in politics is another symptom of this condition.

In the early stages of independence, criollo leaders repressed their sense of guilt by seeking an egalitarian break with the paternal colonial past. Moved by utopian euphoria, these leaders adopted republican-democratic institutions which were ill-suited to the conditions of Spanish America. The elimination of the King, and his replacement by the republican nation-state, created a profound psychological division in Spanish American life. As has been stated, society and the family were still paternal, while national political institutions were, at least nominally, republican-democratic. The history of independent Spanish America has largely been an attempt to reconcile two conflicting components of the cultural psyche-- paternal authoritarianism and liberal institutions.

To bridge this pathological dichotomy, and to repress guilt as well as disorder, other father-figures emerged in nineteenth-century Spanish America. Yet, these figures--caudillos, clergy, and criollo oligarchy--were not newcomers on the scene; they represented throwbacks to colonial paternalism. To replace the royal father, the national caudillos moved into the vacuum created by the loss of kingship. They were at once authoritarian and popular with the masses. Like society at large, they were paternalistic. In their hands, alien liberal institutions were mere toys, to be used as the facade for paternal authoritarianism.

The political scientist, George I. Blanksten, has called the national caudillo "a monarch in republican dress."[5] However, whereas the royal father had ruled by divine sanction, precedent, and, more importantly, habit, the national caudillos ruled by force and personal charisma. This explains the turmoil of the first half of the nineteenth century, when force rather than habit determined the tenure of the new father-figures. Under these conditions, parties, ideologies, platforms, interest-groups, the paraphernalia of republican-democracy, were all largely irrelevant. Pathological instability took hold in the land, as new contenders vied for power.

Although the royal father was gone, the Catholic Church continued to preach obedience to God, the Father, and to the patrilineal family. However, the Church was caught in the political storm of virtual anarchy. Some caudillos viewed the Church as a paternal tool in fostering mass obedience to their own authority. Others, jealous of the Church's influence and alleged material wealth, attacked the institution as a threat to their own power or as an obstacle to the modern state. In general, the Church veered to conservative strongmen in its own quest for a replacement for the royal father.

Nowhere was paternalism as enduring as on the haciendas, the large tracts of land owned by the criollo oligarchy since early colonial times. The nineteenth-century hacendado ruled his estate with the iron fist of paternalism. He was the miniature yet ruthless replacement of the royal father, exploiting the peons through the practice of debt-peonage. Like some conservative thinkers, the agrarian masses might well have rued the passage of royal paternalism. For the overthrow of kingship rendered them vulnerable to the unchecked authority of the hacendado.

It is clear, then, that neither the caudillos nor the clergy nor the hacendados adequately filled the void left by the passing of royal authority. Meanwhile, the republican nation-state, an artificial appendage of society, was rooted in neither popular support nor the paternal conditioning of the masses. Some there were who addressed themselves to this problem. In the political ideas of conservative thinkers, there was an unconscious reminiscence for the days of royal fatherhood. They sought to replace the royal father through strong presidentialism, centralized rule, and Catholic doctrine.

At first sight, history seems to have favored conservative thought. For, in the late nineteenth and early twentieth centuries, strong presidents emerged as the rulers of the Spanish American nations. The growth of international trade, the commercialization of agriculture, and the discovery of vital mineral wealth, all of these placed taxable resources in the hands of chief executives. With new wealth, the presidents organized professional armies which eliminated the local caudillos. Railroads were also built, binding the nation and sending liberal federalism into permanent eclipse. Again constitutionalism and liberalism lost out.

But these new national dictators proved to be inept replacements for royal paternalism. Their paternalism was directed towards immediate political support rather than the protection and benefit of the masses. Power for the sake of power was the aim of the national dictators. Obedience to the criollo oligarchy was their tactic.

During the initial decades of the twentieth century, industrialization and urbanization accomplished what many decades of history failed to achieve--the weakening of the patrilineal family. "Large cities," William L. Schurz has written, "are the natural enemy of the traditional Latin American family."[6] Within the growing cities, the new modes of living proved incompatible with the old ways. The "big houses" of the patrilineal family had once housed sons and daughters, grandparents, relatives, and servants. Married sons and their brides also lived under the watchful eye of the father. The patriarchal home had once served as "an hotel, a court of domestic relations, and a social security system."[7] In the overcrowded cities, however, Spanish Americans were forced into small apartments; sons and daughters left the stern rule of the father; and the political party and trade union vied for the attention of a new generation.

The passing of traditional society in the cities, and the consequent disintegration of the patrilineal family, seemed to dissolve the historic longing for paternal rule. Nationalism, industrialization, public education, and the welfare state stripped the patrilineal family of many of its functions. In many cases, the family's functions were reduced to raising children and influencing the early relations between the sexes. The rise of middle-sector political parties, in alliance with urban workers, seemed to hold out new hope for liberal institutions.

But state paternalism could not replace the longing for the paternal father-figure in the countryside and in the shacks of misery which rimmed the cities. In what may be considered a "return of the repressed," the peons, whether agrarian or uprooted, still yearned for the paternalism of the royal father. Demagogues were quick to exploit this atavistic longing. During the 1920's and 1930's, as nascent democracy foundered on the Great Depression, the armed forces began to deliver new "saviors" to the political scene. The military later became the source of such dictators as Marcos Pérez Jiménez, Gustavo Rojas Pinilla, Juan D. Perón, all of whom rose on the ruins of liberal institutions. In their place, these dictators strove to revive the paternalism and authoritarian father-images of colonial times. As representatives of the armed forces, one of the last bulwarks of the traditional family, these dictators mobilized the uprooted peons. Having recently arrived from the backlands, where paternalism and the patrilineal family still held sway, these peons were prepared to serve their new patrons. The recent efforts to restore these dictators, and the current popularity of military dictators, may be considered as a throwback to the days when royal absolutism provided a father-figure for all Spanish Americans.

Notes

1. See Bruce Mazlish, _The Riddle of History: The Great Speculators from Vico to Freud_ (New York: Harper and Row, 1966), Chapter XI.

2. Philip Rieff, "The Meaning of History and Religion in Freud's Thought," in Bruce Mazlish, ed., _Psychoanalysis and History_ (New York: Grosset and Dunlap, 1971), pp. 23-44.

3. See Sigmund Freud, _Moses and Monotheism_ (New York: Vintage Books, 1967), pp. 101-117.

4. Richard Graham, _Independence in Latin America_ (New York: Alfred A. Knopf, 1972), pp. 6-7.

5. George I. Blanksten, _Ecuador: Constitutions and Caudillos_ (New York: Russell and Russell, Inc., 1964), p. 34.

6. William L. Schurz, _This New World_ (New York: E. P. Dutton, 1964), p. 325.

7. _Ibid._

III

Rebellion, Alienation, and Conformity
in the Lives of the Caudillos:
A Hypothesis

There is, to date, little agreement on the defi-
nition of a caudillo. Nineteenth-century caudillism
has been defined by one historian as "a means for the
selection and establishment of political leadership
in the absence of a social structure and political
groupings adequate to the functioning of representative government." The caudillos, Spanish America's
own brand of dictators, "were the natural leaders of
a society whose colonial order was destroyed before
the bases for an independent society had taken firm
shape."[1] Jesús de Galíndez, however, has written that
caudillism "was not a political concept but a psychological type."[2]

In any case, many social scientists have doubted
that common denominators can be found for the Spanish-
American caudillos. As the political scientist Alexander T. Edelmann has written, "they [the caudillos]
present a frustrating record for any student of political leadership who hopes to classify his specimens
and reach some definite, irrefutable conclusions. For
the caudillos have been a heterogeneous lot, possessing
many contrasting characteristics of all shades and
colors."[3] Other scholars support Edelmann's pessimism
on the possibility of generalizing about caudillos.
"The varieties of civilian caudillos in the nineteenth
century," writes historian John J. Johnson, "were so
numerous that it is virtually impossible to find a common denominator for them."[4] According to historian
Edwin Lieuwen, "the differences [between caudillos]
were often as striking as similarities."[5] Finally,
sociologist Jacques Lambert has written that "it would
be useless to sketch the portrait of the typical
caudillo and paint it black or white."[6]

In the face of such pessimism, the would-be gen-
eralizer can draw some encouragement from the writings
of political scientist Harold D. Lasswell. He has
written, with reference to revolutionary leadership
around the world, that "there are many indications
that the pursuit of power rather than other value out-
comes is to be understood by examining the vicissi-
tudes of early experience in the family or intimate

circle...."[7] In this essay I examine the early experiences in the family during the formative years of the
nineteenth-century caudillos. In analyzing the biographies of one or more caudillos from sixteen nations
of mainland Spanish America, I searched for some pattern of early behavior.

The result of this preliminary analysis is an
hypothesis summed up by the triad, "Rebellion, Alienation, and Conformity," to suggest a possible life cycle
in the biographies of the nineteenth-century caudillos.
An examination of the early lives of the caudillos indicates a high degree of juvenile rebellion against
parental and other authority-figures. Furthermore, it
reveals that among young caudillos who did not overtly
rebel, there were many who were alienated from their
families at an early age. Having broken with, or become estranged from, parental or other authority-figures
in their youths, many of the caudillos were "misfits"[8]
who sought power as a source of personal identity.

The term "misfits," used in a non-pejorative sense
in this essay, refers not to a psychological type but
to a psychological state rooted in the early experience
of the caudillos. Deprived of family identification,
or estranged from parental authority or other sources
of identity such as education, these "misfits" sought
power and social status in a society dominated by the
creole oligarchy. Therefore, the nation-state, a rela-
tively new source of wealth, power, and prestige, became a major preserve of the caudillos. As a cosmopol-
itan elite, preoccupied with local and especially international matters, the creole oligarchy was willing
to rule through these power-seeking "misfits." As for
the caudillos, identification with the creole elite
brought them the kind of status they cherished.

Young Rebels and Alienated Youths

The very personification of nineteenth-century
caudillism was Antonio López de Santa Anna, who ruled
Mexico eleven times between 1832 and 1855. Santa Anna
was born in Jalapa, Vera Cruz, on February 21, 1794,
of middle-class Spanish parents. Santa Anna's father
wanted him to pursue a commercial career and appren-
ticed him to a merchant. But young Santa Anna proved
rebellious. Although he worked for a while in the
store of one José Cos in Vera Cruz, Santa Anna did not
last very long in this position. To the dismay of his
parents, from his boyhood he had been drawn, in his

22

own words, toward "the glorious career of arms, feeling it to be my true vocation and calling."[9] His ambition for a military career was not to be denied, and in 1810 he joined an infantry regiment of the royal army in Mexico.[10]

Rafael Carrera, who ruled Guatemala from 1838 to 1865, was a mestizo peon, more Indian than white. Carrera was born into an impoverished family of Guatemala City. The story of Carrera's early career is one of alienation from his downtrodden family and people. He began life as a poor peon and rose up to the position of swineherd in his young manhood. Carrera was introduced into white society by a priest, who made him a protegé and arranged a marriage for him above his station in life.[11] Deeply religious and intensely ambitious, Carrera never forgot his debt to the priest. His early acceptance into white society, and consequent alienation from his race and family, are keys to understanding Carrera's later political role in Guatemalan history.

José Antonio Páez, ruler of Venezuela from 1830 to 1846, and again from 1861 to 1863, was also separated from his family at an early age. In June, 1807, Páez, then seventeen years old, was sent on an errand to the family lawyer. On the way, he was confronted by robbers, and the young José killed one of his assailants. Páez, who in his own words, was induced by a "puerile fear" to go into hiding, took up the cowboy's way-of-life.[12] "At last, tormented by his fears," writes R. B. Cunninghame Graham, "he left the district, and set his face towards the Llanos, where then as now, a man may hide himself from the whole world. At a great cattle ranch called La Calzada, belonging to one Leon Manuel Pulido, he engaged himself at a salary of three dollars monthly, as a cattle peon. This determination of the young adventurer affected his whole life and all his subsequent career."[13]

Rafael Núñez, who dominated Colombia in the 1880s, was another kind of young man. A nervous youth, reared by his loving mother Dolores, Rafael resented the domination of his father Colonel Francisco Núñez.[14] Looking back at his youth, an aging Rafael remarked to his secretary: "My father was a man of strong character. I don't remember having ever received a kiss from him."[15] In rebellion against the stern upbringing of his father, young Núñez turned to romantic poetry and philosophical radicalism. He became an ideological rebel in his youth, reading deeply in the socialistic principles of Louis Blanc and Saint Simon.[16]

Juan José Flores, ruler of Ecuador from 1830 to 1845, was a product of the army. Born in Puerto Cabello in 1800, Juan's parents are unknown and were most certainly poor people. During his childhood, Flores wandered the streets selling cigarettes. Lacking in education and sensing opportunities in the war for independence, young Juan ran away from the poverty of his home for a new life in the royal army.[17]

Gabriel García Moreno, who ruled Ecuador from 1861 to 1865 and 1869 to 1875, was born on December 24, 1821, into an aristocratic family. A timid child, young Gabriel was dominated by a father he hated. His father, determined to make a man out of his son, sought to drive fear out of Gabriel's system. One day, in the midst of a hurricane, the elder García trapped young Gabriel on the balcony, refused to let him flee, and made him face the violent elements. This event, involving alienation from a domineering father, had a traumatic effect on Gabriel.[18] Gabriel, a studious boy, retreated into fantasy and dreamed of power as an Adlerian compensation for helplessness.[19] Young Gabriel was destined to find a new father-figure in the God of Catholicism.

Andrés Santa Cruz, ablest of the early caudillos and ruler of both Bolivia and Peru, was born about 1794, the son of a Spanish nobleman and an Incan noblewoman. As a youth Andrés father sent him to Cuzco to study in the prestigious Seminario Conciliar de Sant Antonio Abad. There he met the elite of Peurvian society. One day in 1809, an incident put an end to Andrés' studies, and drove a wedge between the youth and his father. As a result of young Santa Cruz's poor academic performance, the superior of the school ordered him confined to his room. Andrés, believing his punishment to be unwarranted, decided to escape. He jumped from his room into the patio, and fled the school forever. At first he sought refuge in the home of the local judge, but, after a few weeks, he returned home defiantly to face his disappointed father.[20]

Mariano Melgarejo, ruler of Bolivia from 1864 to 1871, was born on April 13, 1820, a product of the illicit love of Ignacia Melgarejo and Lorenzo Valencia. His father was a drunkard and his mother, fearing exposure of her love-child, tried to hide the illegitimate cholo boy. Although she pampered Mariano during his childhood, Ignacia finally gave him over to her uncle, a local priest. Padre Rojas set to work to educate and give him religious instruction. But young Mariano preferred drinking, fighting, stealing, and successive love affairs. He soon rebelled against the authority of the priest. Irresistible to women, a favorite at fiestas, Mariano needed money and began to steal the silver from his protector's home. His uncle Rojas pleaded with Mariano to change his ways. But to no avail. "The tiger's cub has begun to show his growing paws."[21]

Diego Portales, who dominated Chile from 1830 to 1837, was also a rebel in his youth. At school young Diego was known for his rebelliousness. In at least one instance, the youth persuaded fellow students to cut classes. Later, in a fit of anger he broke all the dishes in the school kitchen so that meals could not be served. Finally, he dressed a mule in the garb of the rector of the school in order to express his disdain.[22] Hence, Diego Portales, the later defender of order and tradition, was in his youth a restless rebel against authority.

In the Argentine case, there are two important examples of juvenile rebellion, but against different sources of authority. The first was young Juan Facundo Quiroga, the future caudillo of La Rioja, later known as the "tiger of the pampas." In young Facundo's case, rebellion was directed against his father and school authorities. In the Quiroga home, young Facundo could never be induced to take his seat at the family table. He had learned the skills and wildness of the gaucho on his father's estancia. His father, hoping to tame the young cowboy, sent him to school in La Rioja. There Facundo became the terror of his schoolmates and a problem to his teachers. One brave teacher attempted to punish him for failure to master a lesson. But Facundo, contemptuous of all discipline, knocked the teacher out of his chair and fled the school to go into hiding. "Was not such a boy," asked Domingo F. Sarmiento, "the embryo chieftain who would afterwards defy society at large?"[23]

Whereas Quiroga rebelled against his father's authority, Juan Manuel de Rosas, tyrant of Argentina from 1829 to 1852, was reared under different circumstances. In the Rozas family it was the mother, Doña Agustina, who was dominant and who thoroughly controlled her husband. Like Quiroga, however, young Juan, independent of spirit, could not cope with authority at school. He insulted his teachers and refused to perform menial labor as part of school discipline. He was sent home to his domineering mother, who tried to discipline her child. But Rosas would not make amends, and his mother locked him in his room and placed him on a bread-and-water diet. Young Rosas escaped, leaving behind the following message: "I leave all that which is not mine." The young rebel soon ceased to spell his last name with a "z" and dropped his mother's name completely.[24] Having broken with his immediate family, young Juan began a new life. He gave up both formal education and city life and took up a position on one of the <u>estancias</u> of his kinsmen the Anchorenas. There he devoted himself fully to the life of a gaucho chieftain. Popular, even famous in the district, he became a leader of the hard-riding gauchos.[25]

José Gaspar Rodríguez de Francia, who ruled Paraguay from 1811 to 1840, was a misanthrope. According to Thomas Carlyle, "the poor creature's whole boyhood was one long lawsuit: Rodríguez Francia against All Persons in general."[26] An episode in José Gaspar's youth throws light on his early character. Young José hated his father and quarreled with him over his mother's estate. The youth gave his father two months to turn over the property. After issuing this command, José Gaspar retired to a small house distant from his paternal home where, following a solitary life, he had no companion but his books. His father eventually surrendered the legacy, but José Gaspar would never forgive him.[27] Years later his father, lying on his death-bed, begged for a reconciliation with his son. José Gaspar flatly refused. The father's illness was intensified by his son's rebelliousness, and the old man was horrified at quitting the world without mutual forgiveness. A few hours before the father breathed his last, members of the Francia family visited José Gaspar and implored him to receive the dying benediction of his father. When told that his father believed that he could not reach heven unless he departed at peace with his son, José Gaspar replied: "then tell my father that I care not if his soul descends to hell."[28] The old man died raving.

There are some exceptions, it should be noted, to the pattern of juvenile rebellion and early alienation in the lives of the national caudillos. For example,

José Artigas, liberator and caudillo of Uruguay, grew
up "wild" on his father's estancia,[29] but unlike Rosas
and Quiroga he did not rebel against parental authority. Antonio Guzmán Blanco, dictator of Venezuela
from 1870 to 1889, was deeply devoted to his father
Antonio Leocadio Guzmán, journalist and politician.
Francisco Solano López, ruler of Paraguay from 1862
to 1870, inherited power from his father Carlos Antonio
López. Despite these and other exceptions, the fre-
quency of early alienation and rebellion remains im-
pressive.

The Quest for Power

The pattern of alienation and rebellion in the
lives of the young national caudiolos must not be dis-
missed simply as cases of sowing wild oats. For the
family in nineteenth-century Spanish America was the
major source of social status and prestige. Rebellion
against father, mother or teacher, or alienation from
these authority-figures, made of the young caudillos
social "misfits." Desperate men, they were prepared
to risk all for the sake of political power.

In search of status and power, the caudillos
sought to identify themselves with the creole oligarchy, the social elite. Caudillos ruled because
they held the balance of power in Spanish America during the nineteenth century. On one hand, they were
aligned with the creole oligarchy, possessors of wealth
and position; and, on the other, through shrewdness and
instinct they were often the heroes of the illiterate
masses. "Caudillos," writes historian Robert L. Gilmore, "came from all levels of society and regularly
made the interests of the upper class their own."[30]
The landed oligarchy, possessors of all that the national caudillos cherished, were quite willing to rule
through these power-seeking "misfits."

The archtype of the opportunistic, power-hungry
caudillo was Santa Anna of Mexico. It will be re-
membered that at the age of fourteen, Santa Anna left
the business world for a career in the military. His
boyhood hero was Bonaparte, and Santa Anna never out-
grew his desire to become the Napoleon of the West.[31]
Through demagoguery, bombast, and personal magnetism,
Santa Anna "became the fetish of the mob."[32] Yet, he
remained a conservative, never directing his popularity and power against the envied Mexican hacendados.

27

When Rafael Carrera took power in Guatemala through his dominion of Indian hordes, it caused great apprehension among the upper-class whites. But Carrera never forgot his early acceptance into white society and the aid given him by the friendly priest. A visitor to Guatemala, John L. Stephens, described the needless fears of the whites on the eve of Carrera's assumption of power: "There seemed ground for the apprehension that the hour of retributive justice was nigh and that a spirit was awakened among the Indians to make a bloody offering to the spirits of their fathers, and recover their inheritance. Carrera was the pivot on which this turned. He was talked of as El rey de los Indios, the king of the Indians....His power to cause the massacre of every white inhabitant, no one denied." But Carrera was "under the dominion of the priests; and his own acuteness told him that he was more powerful with the Indians themselves while supported by the priests and the aristocracy than at the head of the Indians only...."[33] During his regime, Carrera strove to make Guatemala what he deemed to be the model of a Catholic society. Carrera, the alienated swineherd, the hero of the Indian masses he privately detested, became a tool of the creole oligarchy and of the high clergy. The cycle of alienation and conformity was completed as Carrera used his power to promote religion, property rights, and the firm control of the Indian masses.[34]

Cowboy heroes such as Páez of Venezuela and Rosas of Argentina were caudillos who served the oligarchy while playing the role of men-of-the-people. Páez, the hero of the llaneros of Venezuela, served the conservative elite as president of that country.[35] Rosas of Argentina deliberately catered to the rural lower class, in order to protect the power and interests of the estancieros of Buenos Aires province. In his own words: "You well know the attitude of the have-nots against the wealthy and powerful. I have always considered it very important to acquire an influence over the poor in order to control and direct them; and at great cost in effort, comfort, and money, I have made myself into a gaucho like them, to speak as they do, to protect them, to become their advocate, and to support their interests."[36] The gaucho way-of-life, which Rosas took up as a rebellious youth, thus helped him in winning the allegiance of the masses and protecting the power of the estancieros.

Flores of Ecuador, the once impoverished cigarette

vendor, used his military power to establish a dictatorship in 1830. Having risen to power through the army, Flores had but one objective: permanent political leadership. He màde altruistic statements, but nothing was changed in the social structure of Ecuador. In spite of Flores' humble beginnings, he soon chose to safeguard the interests of the creole oligarchy.[37]

Two of our caudillos, both dominated by overbearing fathers in their youths, found a benevolent father-figure in the God of Catholicism. They also used religion as an instrument of political control. Upon coming to power in the 1880s, Núñez, the young socialist dreamer of Colombia, aligned himself with the clergy, the conservative oligarchy, and the military. He became a "theocratic Ceasar," using religion as an instrument of order.[38] García Moreno of Ecuador, the timid child, grew up to an an "active mystic."[39] Himself an aristocratic, intensely religious leader, García Moreno used Catholicism as a unifying force in Ecuador. He recognized that it was too early to rule by using nationalism as a means to unity.[40]

Bolivia was ruled by two different cholos in the nineteenth century. Santa Cruz, proud of the Inca blood in his veins, was one of the few caudillos to attempt to aid the Indian masses.[41] The bastard, Melgarejo, instituted one long rampage (1864 to 1871), during which time he drank, loved, stole, and killed indiscriminately. In his case, the rebellious tiger cub grew into the wild beast. Neither of these cholos, no matter how popular their origins, challenged the dominance of the creole oligarchy.

Diego Portales, rebel in his youth, became an arch-conservative when he dominated Chile in the years 1830 to 1837. Portales, a self-made man who had built a lucrative trading business by age twenty-three, had nothing but contempt for the masses. "The people," said this new guardian of order, "must be given bread and blows."[42] Portales completed the cycle of youthful rebellion and adult conformity by becoming a firm believer in oligarchical control.

In his youth, Francia of Paraguay showed promise of becoming a champion of the common man.' As a practicing lawyer, Francia became the "friend of the underdog," defending the rights of the Guaraní Indians, who viewed him as a virtual demigod.[43] After he gained power, however, Francia became an iron-fisted dictator who isolated Paraguay from the rest of the world. There is no evidence that Francia's early idealism, which virtually coincided with his youthful rebelliousness, was ever directed against the landed elite in Paraguay.

Conclusion: Caudillos and Society

Social mobility was limited in nineteenth-century Spanish America. Land, the chief source of wealth and status, was mainly in the hands of the creole oligarchy and foreign enterprises. But if Spanish America was dominated by a colonial economy, it was also divided into legally sovereign nation-states with lucrative governmental and military posts. It is therefore not surprising that the nation-state served as one of the targets for ambitious social "misfits," who, having defied parents or been alienated from the family, saw political power as a means for establishing their identity. These were the national caudillos, who, in search of wealth, power, and status, were willing to risk all in order to gain control of the nation-states through coups and violence.[44]

The question may be raised as to why the creole oligarchy, the so-called "natural aristocracy," did not attempt themselves to seize control of the new nation-states of Spanish America. This may be answered by combining several historical factors. First, the national caudillos, who were not reluctant heroes, possessed a virtual monopoly of force in the decades prior to the formation of professional armies.[45] Second, though many were popular figures, the national caudillos were not interested in changing the conventional socio-economic bases of power, and, therefore, posed no threat to the creole elite.[46] Third, as this study has suggested, the national caudillos were, in the main, social "misfits," who sought to attain social status precisely through association with the creole oligarchy. In this respect, the national caudillos served as a conservative force in nineteenth-century Spanish America, binding together the nation, serving as a lightening-rod for popular discontent, and obeying their social superiors dutifully.

Notes

1. Robert L. Gilmore, _Caudillism and Militarism in Venezuela, 1810-1910_ (Athens, Ohio: Ohio University Press, 1964), pp. 47, 50-51.

2. Jesús de Galíndez, _Iberoamérica, su evolución política, socio-económica, cultural y internacional_ (New York: Las Americas, 1954), p. 199.

3. Alexander T. Edelmann, _Latin American Government and Politics_ (Homewood, Illinois: Dorsey, 1965), p. 306.

4. John J. Johnson, _The Military and Society in Latin America_ (Stanford, Cal.: Stanford University Press, 1964), p. 40.

5. Edwin Lieuwen, _Arms and Politics in Latin America_ (rev. ed., New York: Praeger, 1965), p. 23.

6. Jacques Lambert, _Latin America: Social Structure and Political Institutions_, Tr. Helen Katel (Berkeley, Cal.: University of California Press, 1967), p. 160.

7. Harold D. Lasswell and Daniel Lerner, eds., _World Revolutionary Elites_ (Cambridge, Mass.: M.I.T. Press, 1965), p. 15.

8. This term was first applied to the caudillos by Charles W. Anderson, _Politics and Economic Change in Latin America_ (Princeton, N.J.: Van Nostrand, 1967), p. 23.

9. Ann Fears Crawford, ed., _The Eagle: The Autobiography of Santa Anna_ (Austin, Tex.: Pemberton, 1967), p. 7.

10. O. L. Jones, Jr., _Santa Anna_ (New York: Twayne, 1968), p. 22.

11. Paul Burgess, _Justo Rufino Barrios: A Biography_ (Philadelphia: Dorrance, 1926), pp. 41-45.

12. José Antonio Páez, _Autobiografica del General José Antonio Páez_ (2 vols., New York: Elliot, 1945), I, 4-5.

31

13. R. B. Cunninghame Graham, José Antonio Páez (London: Heineman, 1929), p. 6.

14. Nicolás del Castillo Mathieu, Biografia de Rafael Núñez (2 vols., Bogotá: Iqueima, 1955), I, pp. 36-43.

15. Joaquin Tamayo, Núñez (Bogotá: Cromos, 1939), p. 15.

16. Francisco García Calderón, Latin America: Its Rise and Progress (London: Fisher Unwin, 1913), p. 208.

17. Luis Martínez Delgado, Hacia Berruecos (Bogotá: Editorial El Gráfico, 1946), p. 134.

18. Roberto Agramonte y Pichardo, Biografia del dictador García Moreno; estudio psicopatalogico y histórico (Havana: Cultural, 1935), p. 25.

19. Ibid., p. 27.

20. Alfonso Crespo, Santa Cruz: El Cóndor Indio (México: Fondo de Cultura Economica, 1944), pp. 26-27.

21. Manuel Rigoberto Paredes, Melgarejo y su tiempo (La Paz: Bolivia, 1962), pp. 24-25.

22. Lewis W. Bealer, "Diego Portales, Dictator and Organizer of Chile" in A. Curtis Wilgus, ed., South American Dictators (New York: Russell and Russell, 1963), pp. 175-176.

23. Domingo F. Sarmiento, Life in the Argentine Republic in the Days of the Tyrants (New York: Collier, 1961), p. 73.

24. Lewis W. Bealer, "Juan Manuel de Rosas" in Wilgus, ed., South American Dictators, p. 105; José M. Ramos Mejía, Rosas y el Doctor Francia (Estudios Psiquiátricos) (Madrid: Editorial América, 1917), p. 148.

25. Bealer, "Juan Manuel de Rosas," p. 106.

26. Thomas Carlyle, "Dr. Francia" in Critical and Miscellaneous Essays: Collected and Republished (4 vols., Boston: Brown and Taggard, 1860), IV, p. 361.

27. Lewis W. Bealer, "Francia, Supreme Dictator of Paraguay" in Wilgus, ed., South American Dictators, p. 60.

28. J. P. and W. P. Robertson, Letters on Paraguay; An Account of Four Years' Residence in that Republic, Under the Government of the Dictator Francia (3 vols., London: John Murray, 1839), II, pp. 297-298.

29. John Street, Artigas and the Emancipation of Uruguay (New York: Cambridge University Press, 1959), pp. 47-49.

30. Gilmore, Caudillism and Militarism in Venezuela, p. 46.

31. Hubert Herring, A History of Latin America (3rd ed., New York: Knopf, 1968), pp. 296-297.

32. García Calderón, Latin America, p. 151.

33. John L. Stephens, Incidents of Travel in Central America, Chiapas, and Yucatan (2 vols., New York: Harper, 1841), II, pp. 135-136.

34. Herring, History of Latin America, p. 473.

35. García Calderón, Latin America, p. 101.

36. James R. Scobie, Argentina: A City and a Nation (New York: Oxford University Press, 1964), pp. 78-79.

37. Lilo Linke, Ecuador: Country of Contrasts (London: Oxford University Press, 1960), p. 23.

38. J. Fred Rippy, "Dictators of Colombia" in Wilgus, ed., South American Dictators, p. 377.

39. Carlos Octavio Bunge, Nuestra América (Ensavo de Psicología Social) (Buenos Aires: Casa Vaccaro, 1918), p. 284.

40. Linke, Ecuador, p. 24.

41. John E. Fagg, Latin America: A General History (2nd ed., New York: Macmillan, 1969), p. 427.

42. Quoted in Herring, History of Latin America, p. 648.

43. Bealer, "Francia," p. 61.

44. Merle Kling, "Towards a Theory of Power and Political Instability in Latin America," _Western Political Quarterly_, vol. IX (March, 1956), pp. 33-35.

45. Lieuwen, _Arms and Politics_, pp. 23-24.

46. Kling, "Towards a Theory of Power," p. 34.

IV

Life Against Death in Mexican History:
A Study of <u>Machismo</u>

Beginning with the publication in 1920 of his
<u>Beyond the Pleasure Principle</u>, Sigmund Freud set forth
a new view of the instinctual life of man. This view
was placed in the context of civilization in Freud's
<u>Civilization and its Discontents</u>. In the latter work,
he declared: "...besides the instinct to preserve
living substance and join it into ever larger units,
there must exist another, contrary instinct seeking
to dissolve these units and to bring them back to
their primaeval, inorganic state. That is to say, as
well as Eros there was an instinct of death. The
phenomena of life could be explained from the concur-
rent or mutually opposing action of these two instincts." With regard to the death instinct, a "fruit-
ful idea was that a portion of the instinct is diverted
towards the external world and comes to light as an
instinct of aggressiveness and destructiveness....At
the same time we can suspect...that the two kinds of
instinct seldom--perhaps never--appear in isolation
from each other, but are alloyed with each other in
varying and very different proportions..."[1]

In Mexico, the life and death instincts have been
"alloyed" in the phenomenon of <u>machismo</u>--the cult of
aggressive masculinity so typical of the nation's
culture and history. Life--self-preservation and
sexuality--has been pitted perpetually against death--
aggressiveness and destructiveness--in the form of
Mexican <u>machismo</u>. From conqueror to caudillo to revolutionary, Mexicans have displayed a headlong charge
from live-giving sexuality to aggression, destruction,
and death. And their biographies are mirrored in the
modern Mexican <u>macho</u>.

The <u>macho</u> is the masculine ideal in Mexican, indeed all of Latin American, culture and society. Re-
gardless of social position, the <u>macho</u> is admired for
his sexual prowess, action-orientation (both physical
and verbal), and various other components. Stidently
masculine, the <u>macho</u> is allegedly sure of himself,
conscious of his inner worth, and prone to gamble
everything on his self-confidence. The <u>macho</u> may express his inner confidence by overt action, as in the
case of caudillos and revolutionaries, or he may do so
verbally, as in the case of a leading intellectual,

lawyer or politician.[2] These, then, are the surface characteristics of <u>macho</u> consciousness; more on the deeper unconscious implications of <u>machismo</u> will follow as we proceed in this analysis.

The behavior pattern known as <u>machismo</u> was imbibed from Spain, and made its way to Mexico via the soldiers and adventurers who participated in the conquest.[3] The Spanish conquerors, the first <u>machos</u>, displayed a manly bravado and aggressiveness which, against all odds, subdued a continent. Having crossed the ocean without women, they manifested a lusty sexuality, mingling readily with the native women. In their manliness, self-confidence, bravery, and lust, the conquistadors established the model of <u>machismo</u> in Mexico. "It is impossible," writes Octavio Paz, "not to notice the resemblance between the figure of the <u>macho</u> and that of the Spanish conquistador. This is the model--more mythical than real--that determines the images the Mexican people form of their men in power: feudal lords, hacienda owners, politicians, generals, captains of industry. They are all <u>machos</u>, <u>chingones</u>."[4]

But along with the vital life-force qualities of the conquerors, came a Spanish preoccupation with death and a tendency to dwell on it "with morbid insistence."[5] The Spanish conquistador, with all of his life energies, was drawn to death like a magnet. In his personality, the life and death instincts were first mingled in Mexican history.

In the settled society of colonial New Spain, the criollos, sons and grandsons of the conquistadors, became pale shadows of their <u>macho</u> forebears. They were a frustrated sector of Mexican society. Their grandfathers had won the land and by their bravery had given the kingdom to Spain. Now, shorn by the crown of effective power, the criollos were reduced to the position of "political eunuchs" in their own land.[6] Whereas the Spaniards had conquered vast territories and civilizations, the criollos concentrated on the conquest of women.[7] The life-force was thus altered, as aggressive sexuality became the major component of the new <u>machismo</u>.

In the conmingling of colonial instincts, death took on an even greater importance. In New Spain, "a man's death was undeniably more important than his birth. It was not a confused performance involving walking on tiptoe and taking off hats, but a translucent

36

event, a glorification, and it behooved a man to meditate on it and prostrate himself on the ground."[8]

Machismo flourished in independent Mexico. From the attainment of independence to the outbreak of the Mexican Revolution in 1910, machismo was firmly imprinted on the character of the nation. Life and death were alloyed in the caudillos and revolutionaries of the period. Caudillos and revolutionary alike personified the sexual aggressiveness, manliness, action-orientation, and daring which intensified the macho ideal in Mexico.[9] In the nineteenth century, Santa Anna, "whose 'way with women' was legendary,"[10] came to embody the ideal of masculine aggressiveness, and his qualities were mirrored in the caudillos who followed.

The Mexican Revolution, which began on November 20, 1910, opened the dikes to an orgy of sexual rampage and destructiveness.[11] Although Pancho Villa, the revolutionary leader of the north, committed many sexual outrages and atrocities in the name of the Revolution, he is renowned today in Mexico as having lived up to the model of "manliness."[12] When in 1911 Francisco Madero proved timid and indecisive (lacking in pantalones) in stopping the warfare raging in the countryside, Villa, from his exile in Texas, advised him that "all you have to do it hitch up your pants and be a man."[13]

Against the background of sexual excesses and destruction of the Mexican Revolution, death took on a new allure; it came to symbolize the new egalitarianism. In death all men, stripped of differences, values, and protestations, "lose the deceit that social conventions lend them."[14] The instinct of death, so apparent in the conquistadors, criollos, and caudillos, thus took on an even greater intensity, even as the Revolution spread hopes of a better day.

The residue of the long history of machismo is evident in the upbringing of the modern Mexican male. In a sense, the male child of Mexico is the living embodiment of centuries of macho leaders. In childhood, there must be no dolls, or doll houses, but soldiers, guns, military helmets, broomstick horses, swords, "titanic yells, imposing screams, panic among the girls." Any manifestation of feminine interests is disapproved of by older brothers, uncles, cousins, and the mother herself. Older children discriminate

against younger ones on the basis that they are not
macho enough to participate in their games which become progressively more "masculine" (rougher and more
aggressive). The macho image is thus perpetuated not
only by parents, but from older to younger children so
that all look forward with longing to the attainment
of greater virility. Little girls are either avoided
or a "steam roller" attitude is assumed towards them
by the growing machos.[15]

During the entire childhood, signs of virility
are courage to the point of temerity, aggressiveness,
and the unwillingness to run away from a fight or
break a deal (no rajarse). When the child reaches
adolescence, the sign of virility is to talk about or
act in the sexual sphere. The leader of the group is
one who possesses knowledge or experience in sexual
matters. From adolescence and throughout the entire
life of the male, virility will be measured by sexual
potential, with physical strength, courage, and auda-
city as secondary factors.[16]

Amidst all this life-force vitality, death remains a major preoccupation. Virility is assured when
the male child "speaks of or actually shows that he is
not afraid of death."[17] "The Mexican...," writes
Octavio Paz, "is familiar with death, caresses it,
sleeps with it, celebrates it; it is one of his favorite toys and his most steadfast love....Our contempt
for death is not at odds with the cult we have made of
it. Death is present in our fiestas, our games, our
loves, and our thoughts. To die and to kill are ideas
that rarely leave us. We are seduced by death."[18]

Beneath the Mexican macho's lust for life and
death, Samuel Ramos has found deep-seated feelings of
inferiority. He uses as his "model" the Mexican
pelado, the city tramp, "for he constitutes the most
elemental and clearly defined expression of national
character." According to Ramos, "he is like a ship-
wreck victim who, after flailing about in a sea of
nothingness, suddenly discovers his driftwood of salvation: virility. The pelado's terminology abounds
in sexual allusions which reveal his phallic obsession;
the sexual organ becomes symbolic of masculine force.
In verbal combat he attributes to his adversary an
imaginary femininity, reserving for himself the masculine role. By this stratagem he pretends to assert his
superiority over his opponent." "The phallus," Ramos
continues, "suggests to the pelado the idea of power.

38

From this he has derived a very impoverished concept of man. Since he is, in effect, a being without substance, he tries to fill his void with the only suggestive force accessible to him: that of the animal."[19]

Octavio Paz finds one of the essences of Mexican machismo in the word "chingar." According to Paz, its "ultimate meaning always contains the idea of aggression, whether it is the single act of molesting, pricking or censuring, or the violent act of wounding or killing. The verb denotes violence, an emergence from oneself to penetrate another by force. It also means to injure, to lacerate, to violate--bodies, souls, objects--and to destroy....The idea of breaking, or ripping open, appears in a great many of these expressions. The word has sexual connotations, but it is not a synonym for the sexual act: one may chingar a woman without actually possessing her. And when it does allude to the sexual act, violation or deception give it a particular shading. The man who commits it never does so with the consent of the chingada. Chingar, then, is to do violence to another. The verb is masculine, active, cruel: it stings, wounds."[20]

If the aggressive macho is the male stereotype in Mexico, the female mariana is his counterpart. "The husband-wife relationship," writes May N. Diaz, "can be characterized as that between the macho, virile, aggressive male, and the mujer abnegada, the self-sacrificing, dutiful woman."[21] There is in Mexico, indeed all of Latin America, universal agreement on what a "real woman" is like and the way she should behave. Semi-divine, morally superior, and spiritually strong, she has an infinite capacity for humility and self-sacrifice. Her self-denial and patience are displayed in her submission to the men-husbands, sons, fathers, brothers. Beneath the submissiveness, however, lies strength, for the Mexican female has learned that men must be humored and are como niños whose intemperance, foolishness, and obstinacy must be forgiven because "they can not help the way they are."[22]

In a sense the Mexican female, and the cult of the Mother in that country, sum up the life and death instincts in machismo. The macho would, in the end, like to love and chingar the mariana. In her forebearance, he finds, love, mystery, and death all at once. Indeed, there is a close relationship between overcompensating aggression and underlying feelings of weakness in the macho's attitude toward the mariana. A popular theme in Mexican music tells of the macho who, having risked his manliness in love, is rejected and kills himself by performing a deed of heroic masculinity. In these songs, he pleads for sympathy from the desired woman. The seemingly contradictory dominance-submission poles of the macho's inferiority complex are manifested in Mariachi songs, which are laced with shouts of despairing wails, and in which the theme of martyrdom and death allow the singer to reveal his unconscious desire to submit to women.[23]

Octavio Paz sees in the macho's aggressiveness the surface characteristic of underlying "homosexual inclinations." He finds such evidence in "the use and abuse of the pistol, a phallic symbol which discharges death rather than life, and the fondness for exclusively masculine guilds."[24] A more apt explanation lies in combining the Freudian concept of bisexuality with the Adlerian concept of the masculine protest. When machismo is highly rated in a culture, a child may see the masculine role as an impossible attainment or come to despise what he considers femininity. In an attempt to cloak his feelings of inferiority or femininity, he may overcompensate through hypermasculine wishes and actions. Macho traits of aggressive masculinity may be compensations for "tendencies toward submission and obedience, which are unconsciously equated with femininity and inferiority." A craving for the satisfaction of macho goals and personal triumphs may lead to defeat, and the consequent magnification of feelings of inferiority and "womanliness."[25]

In this syndrome, death takes on a new meaning. It is the ultimate flight from femininity, and its acceptance the ultimate test of masculinity. In proving his manly acceptance of death, the macho passes the final test in the struggle between masculine and feminine drives.

Since the Revolution, a change has occurred in Mexican machismo. The violence and aggressiveness so typical of that stage has given way to intransigence as the major characteristic of machismo. Make no mistake, to be politically powerful in Mexico still means to be "male," to assume the "macho" role.[26] But behind the macho intransigence--the manly president and the obedient followers of PRI--the Mexican system of government has shown a new openness to what is considered the "feminine" characteristic of maneuvering and petitioning.[27] The dominant, manly president now

40

bends to the winds of compromise and reconciliation.

National character, if it indeed exists, can be the rock upon which a society endures or splits apart. Whether Mexican society, subject to such strains in the present, will endure in the future will depend, in large part, on the recognition that life is compromise --between liberty and authority, between dominance and submission, and between masculinity and femininity. The macho will always exist in Mexican society. But if the Mexicans adapt their character to the needs of a society in rapid transition, they may "no longer need to learn how to die; they may now even plan how to live."[28]

Notes

1. Sigmund Freud, *Civilization and Its Discontents*, Trans. James Strachey (New York: Norton, 1961), pp. 65-66.

2. John Gillin, "Ethos Components in Modern Latin American Culture," *American Anthropologist*, vol. 57, no. 3 (June, 1955), p. 493.

3. Jon M. White, *Cortés and the Downfall of the Aztec Empire* (New York: St. Martin's Press, 1971), p. 327.

4. Octavio Paz, *The Labyrinth of Solitude: Life and Thought in Mexico*, Trans. Lysander Kemp (New York: Grove Press, 1961), p. 82.

5. William L. Schurz, *This New World* (New York: Dutton, 1964), p. 83.

6. *Ibid.*, pp. 311-312.

7. Aniceto Aramoni, *Psicoanálisis de la dinámica de un pueblo* (México: Universidad Nacional Autonoma de México, 1961), p. 132.

8. Fernando Benítez, *The Century After Cortés*, Trans. Joan MacLean (Chicago: The University of Chicago Press, 1965), p. 69.

9. Aramoni, *Psichoanálisis*, p. 140.

10. Ann Fears Crawford, ed., *The Eagle: The Autobiography of Santa Anna* (Austin: The Pemberton Press, 1967), p. xii.

11. Aramoni, *Psicoanálisis*, p. 140.

12. Frederick C. Turner, *The Dynamic of Mexican Nationalism* (Chapel Hill: The University of North Carolina Press, 1968), p. 110.

13. Evelyn P. Stevens, "Mexican Machismo: Politics and Value Orientations," *Western Political Quarterly*, vol. 18, no. 4 (December, 1965), p. 850.

14. Turner, *The Dynamic of Mexican Nationalism*, p. 292.

15. Rogelio Diaz-Guerrero, "Neurosis and the Mexican Family Structure," _American Journal of Psychiatry_, vol. 112, no. 6 (December, 1955), p. 411.

16. _Ibid._, p. 412.

17. _Ibid._

18. Paz, _The Labyrinth of Solitude_, pp. 57-58.

19. Samuel Ramos, _Profile of Man and Culture in Mexico_, Trans. Peter G. Earle (Austin: The University of Texas Press, 1962), pp. 58-61.

20. Paz, _The Labyrinth of Solitude_, pp. 76-77.

21. May N. Diaz, _Tonalá: Conservatism, Responsibility, and Authority in a Mexican Town_ (Berkeley and Los Angeles: University of California Press, 1966), p. 78.

22. Evelyn P. Stevens, "Marianismo: The Other Face of Machismo in Latin America," in Ann Pescatello, ed., _Female and Male in Latin America: Essays_ (Pittsburgh: University of Pittsburgh Press, 1973), pp. 94-95.

23. Carl E. Batt, "Mexican Character: An Alderian Interpretation," _Journal of Individual Psychology_, vol. 5, no. 2 (November, 1969), pp. 189-190.

24. Paz, _The Labyrinth of Solitude_, p. 82.

25. Batt, "Mexican Character," p. 188.

25. Diaz, _Tonalá_, p. 108.

27. Stevens, "Mexican Machismo," pp. 853-854.

28. T. B. Irving, "Introduction" to Ramos, _Profile of Man and Culture in Mexico_, p. xix.

V

Dichotomies of Militarism in Argentina*

S. E. Finer, the English expert on that worldwide phenomenon, militarism, recently described the various positions taken by the Argentine military during the last forty years. "The Argentine military," he wrote, "have in turn allied themselves with the estancieros, with organized labor, with the Radical middle classes, and many among the azules are prepared to ally themselves with labor again." Finer used the Argentine case to bolster his contention that Latin American military men are motivated mainly by "corporate bias" and that, in the last analysis, they are "'for themselves alone.'" The "primal claim" of the Latin American military establishment "is the perpetuation and security of its existence and status. To this end it shows an almost chemical affinity to whatever social force or political movement will guarantee its power."[1] Class bias, the quest for social mobility, and institutional tradition are important in the motivation of military men. But, above all, "corporate bias" and institutional opportunism determine the political actions of the armed forces.

There is undoubtedly a large kernel of validity in Finer's thesis. Corporate interests have been more important than class bias in shaping the various political positions of the largely middle-class Argentine army officer corps. However, among these corporate interests are certain values that transcend the ever-present drives for security, power, status, pay and armaments. Institutional opportunism will not suffice to explain the seemingly divergent political stances taken by the Argentine army since 1930. As the sociologist, José Luis de Imaz, has written, the military in Argentina is a "power factor" with permanent objectives and values. These values are expressed when the army moves into recurrent crises of legitimacy in a fragmented society.[2]

Many of the seemingly divergent political positions taken by the Argentine army in the past are attributable to a dichotomy in institutional values.

---

*Reprinted from Orbis, Volume X, Fall 1966, Number 3, pp. 930-939.

The Argentine army is at once a traditional and a modern institution, and it is torn by these conflicting values. On the one hand, the Argentine army officer has been inculcated with respect for tradition, a simple patriotism, a gentlemanly Catholicism, and a desire for social order. On the other hand, he has been driven by a modern nationalism that derives from his technical-military functions. This nationalism calls for autarchy, industrialization and technological modernization to build the economic base of a strong war machine. Yet, such modernization bring in its wake social changes that collide with and erode traditional values. Industrialization, for example, promotes the growth of new social and political forces, is accompanied by economic strife, weakens the patrilineal family, and in general attacks the values of the past. How to reconcile its traditional value-structure with the requirements and effects of modernization has been a fundamental dilemma of the Argentine army. This dichotomy of values may serve as one integrating hypothesis in explaining the tortuous course of militarism in Argentina.

I

The history of Argentine militarism is largely the history of army factions, not of a politically monolithic officer corps. Modern militarism emerged in the revolution of 1930, which was executed by two minority factions of the army. The overthrow of Radical President Hipólito Yrigoyen in 1930 was one of the crucial turning-points in Argentine history. Most of the army officer corps, middle class and pro-Radical, did not actively support the revolution. Their inaction was, in part, a result of the traditional-modern dichotomy of values. On the one hand, they were repelled by the ineptitude of the senile President's regime, the squabbling of political factions in congress, the paralysis of the government in the face of economic depression, and the neglect of the technical needs of the armed forces. On the other, they had been drawn to the Yrigoyen regime by its middle-class origins, its support of economic nationalism, and its dedication to an independent foreign policy. The failure of middle-class Radicalism to provide a civilian vehicle for the nationalism of the army is a key concept in understanding the course of Argentine militarism.

The two rival factions that overthrew Yrigoyen were led by Generals José F. Uriburu and Agustín P.

Justo, respectively. The Uriburu faction sought to combine military rule, political authoritarianism and economic nationalism. Traditional values of social order and elite rule, and modern drives for industrialization, protectionism and economic nationalism were to be reconciled under the rule of a military strong man. That Uriburu espoused fascist pretensions only underscores the drive to attain economic modernization while coping with its social repercussions by force. In 1930 these views were too radical for most of the army officer corps. While Uriburu was serving as provisional president (1930-1931), his rival for revolutionary leadership, General Justo, gained control of the army by forging an uneasy alliance between his own "justista" faction and Radical officers known as the "legalists." Confronted by rising military opposition, Uriburu was forced to hold presidential elections in 1931, in which Justo emerged as the victor by fraud and electoral manipulation.

The "justista-legalist" alliance broke down soon after Justo took office in 1932. His regime, dependent largely on the old conservative, free-trading oligarchy for civilian support, soon alienated the pro-Radical "legalists." The Justo regime launched the so-called infamous decade (1932-1943), which witnessed the restoration of rule by the conservative oligarchy, electoral fraud, governmental corruption, and the opening of Argentina to foreign investors. During this period, nationalistic army officers lost faith in professional politicians of every stripe. Enraged by the "sell-out" of the nation to foreign interests in league with the oligarchy, they found no outlet for their nationalism in the Radical Party.

So again Radicalism--divided in tactics, rent by feuds over leadership, excluded from power by corruption--proved inept as a civilian vehicle for army nationalism. Furthermore, because many of the active "legalists" had been purged from the army as a result of unsuccessful uprisings from 1932 to 1934, Radicalism had lost much of its influence in the military. Hence, neither the civilian oligarchy nor the middle class could satisfy the army's desire for social order and modernization. Given the choice between the "justista" faction, and its alliance with the free-trading oligarchy, and the "uriburuista" brand of supernationalistic militarism, most army officers opted for the latter. The lack of a legitimate political outlet for their values led them again, in 1943, to seize the

47

state in an effort to promote social order, traditional values and economic modernization by authoritarian means.

II

The traditional-modern dichotomy within the army was dramatized by the decrees issued after the seizure of the state in 1943. Social order was to be established by dissolving the "babbling" political parties, regulating the press, and placing severe restraints on labor unions. Religious, or Catholic, teaching was made obligatory in the schools. Morals were to be regulated by decrees upholding traditional values. Respect for God, country and family became the ideals of education. Paralleling this drive for social order and traditionalism was the campaign to convert Argentina into a modern industrial state. Expanded government control over the economy featured a policy of autarchy and forced industrialization designed to defend Argentina from economic fluctuations beginning outside the nation. Tariffs were raised, new factories were built under military supervision, and labor was ordered to serve and obey in the interest of economic development.

The army nationalists who seized the state in 1943 honored the memory of Uriburu for having "led the liberating movement" of 1930. However, one among them, Colonel Juan D. Perón, was not prepared to repeat Uriburu's error of basing a nationalistic military regime on such slim pillars as fascistoid intellectuals, provincial elites and some members of the clergy. A shrewd student of Argentine history, Perón recognized that the army nationalists could not hold power for long without the legitimizing force of substantial civilian support. To the traditionalist forces of the regime--the army, fascist-sympathizing elites and some members of the clergy--must be added a largely untapped social force. Thus it was that Perón (1943-1946), in a move deemed unusual for an army officer, began to court the descamisados, the laboring masses. Like the army, labor had not found an outlet for its demands in the established political parties. Perón was able to harness labor to the regime, thus converting it from a military to a majoritarian dictatorship. He forged an army-worker alliance, which promoted his personal ambitions, legitimized military rule, and promised control of the effects of modernization by an authoritarian state. Viewed from this standpoint, Peronism initially represented an effort to bridge the traditional-modern

48

dichotomy through controlled "massification" of an army revolution.

As supporters of the Perón dictatorship (1946-1955), army officers were torn by an ambivalence rooted in the traditional-modern dichotomy of values. They were gratified by their role in running the state and the economy, but restive under the alliance with labor. The role of Eva Perón in inciting the masses to political action violated their traditionalist view of the role of women in Argentine society. It aroused their antipathy toward the demagogic promotion of social strife over social order. They were also wary lest labor become too strong and begin to control the regime. Perón's programs for industrialization, economic nationalism and military modernization pleased them. Yet they felt that certain civilian economic advisers, like Miguel Miranda, wielded too much influence on the regime and were prone to favor light industry over the heavy industries necessary for the military machine. Army officers were further pleased by Perón's support for the Church and his schemes to expand Argentine influence in Latin America. At the same time, they recognized that Peronist doctrine ("justicialism") might enter into active competition with traditional values of patriotism and Catholicism.

Although there were always rumblings of discontent in the army, these did not reach serious proportions until 1951. That year marks another significant turning-point in Argentine politico-military history. By 1951 Perón could no longer buy the support of both pillars of the regime--army and labor. His economic policies had undermined the exchange-earning power of the agrarian sector, and inflation and deterioration began to set in. In 1951 the army took its stand against the vice-presidential ambitions of Eva and against the possibility of a woman becoming commander-in-chief. Perón's support in the Church was also weakening over issues such as educational ordeals and control of charity. Against this backdrop of growing discontent, there occurred a premature uprising of army units under General Benjamín Menéndez. Easily suppressed, the rebellion was nevertheless indicative of widespread restiveness in the army. Subsequent investigations smashed large-scale military conspiracies led by General Eduardo Lonardi and Colonel José F. Suárez in February 1952.

During the period 1952 to 1955, Perón moved

49

toward a totalitarianism that violated both the traditional and modern values of the army. Whereas previously he had sought to divide, manipulate, bribe and cater to the army, now he sought to dominate and remold that traditional institution. This move was made necessary by the growing economic weakness of the dictatorship, which could no longer finance the demands of the two pillars of power. From 1952 to 1955, economic weakness forced Perón into a rapprochement with the United States, climaxed by the hated contract with Standard Oil in 1955.

Perón had thus betrayed army nationalism. For nationalist army officers, this betrayal came on the heels of a program to indoctrinate the whole institution of the military with justicialist ideals, thus threatening its traditional value-structure. Loyalty to the Peronist state was to become the leading value on all levels of the military, superseding loyalty to institution and to historic Fatherland. Perón's attack on the Church in 1954 gave further proof of his totalitarian intentions and of his desire to bend all traditional institutions--army, Church, and even family--to his will. Finally, owing to intense opposition aroused by an abortive naval uprising in June 1955, Perón threatened to arm and unleash the descamisado horde. This threat to organize and arm labor militias challenged the military's traditional control over the organized force of the nation.

Perón's drive toward totalitarianism sparked an alliance uniting a small sector of the army officer corps, the conservative navy, and the air force, which overthrew Perón in the "Liberating Revolution" of September 1955. Significantly, Perón responded to that crisis with the same traditional-modern dichotomy of values which has plagued the Argentine army officer since 1930. Preoccupied with social order rather than social revolution, he was unwilling to alter the nature of his regime by making good his threat to arm the descamisados and hurl them against the military rebels. It is true that army officers loyal to the dictatorship resisted this move as detrimental to their own interests. Yet there is no doubt that Perón faced the crisis with the army nationalist's traditional inclination for social order over the chaos of violent revolution. In the end, the army officer's conditioning won out over that of the demagogic leader of the masses.

III

The "Liberating Revolution" had halted Perón's drive to convert a majoritarian dictatorship, built on both traditional and modern forces, into a totalitarian regime with justicialism as the official doctrine of an all-powerful state. Perón had betrayed army nationalism. The army, which had gambled on big government and big labor to satisfy its conflicting drives, had gotten its fingers burnt. Perón was gone, but the lusty remnants of Peronism survived. Peronists controlled labor, the first mass party in Argentine history, and the largest and most coherent voting bloc (30 to 40 percent of the voters). With the military in control in 1955, one question eclipsed all others: how to deal with Peronism? The answer came from a militant minority in the armed forces, comprised of the _revanchista_ faction of 1951, junior army officers and the conservative navy. This coalition, favoring a hard-line policy toward Peronism, ousted the caretaker government of General Eduardo Lonardi (September-November 1955), who was deemed too soft on the followers of the ex-dictator. General Pedro E. Aramburu was installed as provisional president (1955-1958), and de-Peronization was imposed on every institution of the nation.

The traditional-modern dichotomy of values was submerged by the tide of postrevolutionary revulsion against Perón. In response to the hard facts of economic life and in reaction against the policies of the fallen dictator, the army forsook the statist approach to technological modernization and economic nationalism. The hard-line anti-Peronists of the army, known initially as the "gorillas," veered toward a traditional conservatism. To rid their institution of the taint of collaboration with the dictatorship, the "gorillas" adopted values diametrically opposed to those held in the past. Against the cult of the totalitarian state, they now responded with economic individualism. Against the demagogic promotion of social welfare, they supported a society that left the solution of such problems to the free interplay of economic forces. Except for economic sectors vital to national defense, such as petroleum, the "gorillas" were prepared to go along with the free economy, private enterprise, and the opening of the nation to foreign investments. For the "gorilla," this meant abandoning statist nationalism for new and freer roads to economic reconstruction. For the Peronist masses, these values signalized the army's return to the "justista" tradition of alliances with the conservative elites and the foreign interests. The army was thus pitted against Peronist labor.

Since 1958 the major dichotomy within the army has not stemmed from established institutional values, but has arisen in response to the overriding issue of Peronism. After all, a Peronist resurgence might carry vengeance in its wake against army officers who had staked their careers and lives in campaigns against the followers of the ex-dictator. One side of the new dichotomy has been represented by the hard-line anti-Peronists, known first as the "gorillas," later as the "interventionists," and today as the colorados (reds). Descended from the revanchista faction of 1951, these coalitions, in league with the conservative navy, have sought to exclude the Peronists from participation in politics. Some of the hard-liners have even favored a military dictatorship that would stamp out Peronism once and for all.

Under Aramburu, the "gorillas" supervised the de-Peronization of the armed forces and other institutions. During the administration of Arturo Frondizi (1958-1962), the "interventionists" blocked all efforts made by the President to integrate the Peronists into the Radical Intransigent Party. Most of the "interventionists" assented to Frondizi's contracts with foreign companies for the exploitation of Argentine petroleum resources, which policy did cause some rumblings of discontent in the army officer corps. But the "interventionists" were far more preoccupied with fears of a Peronist resurgence than with the possibility of foreign control of resources vital to defense. When in March 1962 the Peronists scored breathtaking victories in gubernatorial and congressional elections, the "interventionists" led the way in overthrowing Frondizi.

During the Frondizi administration, another coalition began to emerge within the army. Led by those officers who supported "Fair Play" in 1958, or the transference of power to Frondizi in spite of his election by Peronist support, this coalition was known as the "legalists." The "legalists" sought to limit military intervention in politics during the Frondizi years. After reluctantly assenting to the ouster of Frondizi in March 1962, they became known as the azules (blues). It was the azules who blocked efforts by the hard-line colorados to establish a military dictatorship after

Frondizi was overthrown. During the interim regime of
José María Guido (1962-1963), the azules came to support civilian rule, the ultimate removal of the army
from politics, and the gradual integration of the
Peronist masses into political life by a process subject to electoral retraints. In a series of contests
for power with the colorados of both the army and navy,
the azules emerged as the dominant coalition in the
armed forces. Their victory paved the way for the
election in 1963 of Arturo Illia, presidential candi-
date of the moderate Popular Radicals.

IV

The commitment of the armed forces to legalism
came to an abrupt end on June 28, 1966 when, after
thirty-two months in office, President Illia was ousted
by a military coup. For military men, the lackluster
Illia regime had come to represent a power vacuum that
threatened their vital interests. Along with general
charges of weakness and the lack of an effective policy,
the military held the Illia administration responsible
for three developments. First, and foremost, was the
resurgence of Peronism. Illia had adopted a policy of
permitting the gradual integration of neo-Peronists
into the institutional structure of Argentina. In the
congressional elections of March 1965, the neo-Peronists
had scored a major victory, gaining 36 percent of the
total vote and tripling their congressional representa-
tion to forty-three deputies. In the months prior to
Illia's overthrow, neo-Peronists had won six of seven
provincial elections, some by heavy pluralities. Military men feared that such gains might continue in congressional and gubernatorial elections scheduled for
March 1967. Each gain made by the neo-Peronists posed
a threat to the military's position as the most influ-
ential "power factor" in Argentine politics.

The second major development that dismayed the
military was a wave of strikes and labor unrest in a
nation beset with deep-seated economic problems, for
which both resurgent Peronism and the weakness of the
Illis regime were held responsible. As early as
February 1964, a special session of congress had
granted the Illia government broad powers to regulate
the production and sale of basic commodities. However, the regime had accomplished little in its efforts
to curb inflation, speculation and corruption. These
economic disorders, combined with the increasing demands of Peronist labor, proved intolerable to the

53

armed forces.

The third development that alienated the military was alleged communist infiltration of the universities. Military men looked upon the universities as the carriers of alien "extremist" ideas and, to a certain extent, as traditional political enemies of the armed forces. As the economy foundered and the discontent of the masses mounted, some of them believed that atheistic, revolutionary communism might spread from the universities to the rest of Argentina.

That the military's top brass selected Lieutenant General Juan Carlos Onganía to rule Argentina in the aftermath of the 1966 coup, indicates strikingly just how fragile was its "legalist" and azul tradition. Prior to the coup, Onganía had built a reputation as a thoroughgoing "legalist" who believed that the armed forces should be removed from politics. Until his retirement in November 1965, he had served as a buffer between the increasingly restive army and the Illia regime.

Now Onganía, aided by a three-man junta representing all branches of the armed forces, has been placed at the helm of a military regime that openly declares the civilians incompetent to rule. At this early date, it is impossible to predict in which direction this regime will move. However, there are signs which indicate that it may represent a revival of the historic army dream of reconciling social order with modernization through authoritarian military rule. The communiqué issued when the military seized power called for "discipline" and "modernization" in Argentina. Furthermore, many of the Argentine officers had been deeply influenced by the example of General Humberto Castelo Branco, who in April 1964 had seized power in Brazil with similar objectives. Finally, the recent police invasions of Argentine universities, ordered by the new Onganía regime as a blow against "extremists," indicate that the military seems willing to sacrifice the nation's brainpower on the altar of "discipline" and "modernization."

V

The traditional-modern dichotomy of values may provide an integrating hypothesis for other case studies of Latin American militarism. For example, as historian Edwin Lieuwen has written, after 1930

Latin American army officers generally began to veer between advocacy of modernization and reform and defense of social order and traditional elites.[3] Such oscillation may, in part, have been attributable to the traditional-modern dichotomy. On the one hand, the army officer favors economic nationalism and technological modernization. On the other, his desire for social order, respect for traditional elites, and attraction to simple values of God, country and patrilineal family all seem threatened by political change and the effects of modernization.

The rise of Fidelism, which carries with it a threat to destroy the professional army, had a profound impact on the thinking of Latin American military men. They saw how Fidelism in Cuba began as a middle-class, reformist-nationalist movement and ended by destroying the traditional pillars of society, including of course the military establishment. Many army officers came to believe that other reformist-nationalist movements in Latin America might open the dikes to Fidelism. Middle-class parties thus became suspect as vehicles for promoting modernization and guaranteeing social order. This, in part, explains the resurgence of militarism and its trend toward the right.

After the recent wave of military coups, some experts on political developments in Latin America began to discern a pattern that they labeled the "new militarism." In this new pattern, the military serves as the bridge between chaotic civilian rule and regimes dedicated to social order and modernization. The pattern begins when Latin American armies intervene as "corporations" rather than as the vehicles of politically ambitious officers. Military intervention is temporary and aims at curbing internal strife in order to re-establish institutions of state. With this accomplished, the armed forces arrange the election of civilian regimes dedicated to both "national security," or the control of leftist extremism, and the modernization of the economy for the ultimate benefit of all. The examples used to support the existence of a "new militarism" are Peru, where President Belaunde Terry has proved acceptable to the army; Brazil, where General Castelo Branco has formed a new "revolutionary party" that will elect his successor in the near future; and Bolivia and Ecuador, where acceptable political formulas are being worked out by the armed forces.[4] Whether the Onganía regime in Argentina will fit this pattern remains to be seen. In the aftermath of the latest coup, rebel Argentine officers expressed harsh disdain for nearly all civilian politicians.

This so-called new militarism probably represents an adaptation of deeply rooted military values to the current Latin American scene. Still torn by the traditional-modern dichotomy of values, Latin American armies are nevertheless assuming the role of the guardians of ordered change. They have increasingly accepted the fact that basic change in Latin America is inevitable, but they are also determined to reconcile economic modernization with social and political order imposed from above. Such determination is, in part, the result of the failure of military men to find adequate civilian vehicles for their goals. For many of them, the spectrum of Latin American politics is represented by backward oligarchies, quarrelsome and sometimes inept middle-class reformist parties, and expectant masses to whom Fidelism and communism make their appeals. In their quest for social order and modernization, the Latin American armies will probably rely increasingly on the new industrial elites that cherish political stability and profit most from economic development. Some of the old oligarchies will no doubt rally to the cause of the military men, if only as a stopgap to the revolutionary deluge that threatens them.[5]

Notes

1. S. E. Finer, "The Argentine Trouble: Between Sword and State," _Encounter_, September 1965, pp. 65-66.

2. José Luis de Imaz, "Los que mandan: las fuerzas armadas en Argentina," _America latina_ (Rio de Janeiro), October-December 1964, p. 40.

3. Edwin Lieuwen, _Arms and Politics in Latin America_ (revised edition, New York: Praeger, 1965), p. 59.

4. Juan de Onis, "New Role Sought by Latin Military," _New York Times_, March 6, 1966, p. 26.

5. As a postscript to this hypothesis, a note on the methodology for the study of Latin American militarism is in order. If institutional values are of considerable importance in shaping the course of Latin American militarism, then social scientists must revise their methodology for analyzing the phenomenon. However important, statistical studies of the social and geographical origins of the officer corps will not suffice. The need is for intensive studies of the military way-of-life, focusing on values produced by institutional conditioning. Only when we know what kind of personality Latin American military training produces will we be able to analyze the phenomenon of militarism in depth.

VI

Political Implications of Middle-Class
Psychology in Latin America

Twenty-one years have passed since the publication of John J. Johnson's seminal book _Political Change in Latin America: The Emergence of the Middle Sectors_.[1] Written at the high tide of reformism in Latin America in the 1950s, this book gave an overly optimistic view of the role of the middle class in the changing politics of the region. Reformism has since then given way to militarism and reaction in Latin America, and the new literature reflects this change. This paper seeks to test the validity of Johnson's theses, using the new literature to analyze the mentality of the Latin American middle class and its implications for politics in the area.

It must first be recognized that the Johnson hypothesis applied a deeply rooted Western concept to a unique social phenomenon in Latin America. The hope that a middle class would moderate the differences between elites and masses goes back to the Greeks and Aristotle. This concept was later applied by classical writers, such as Polybius and Livy, who used it to explain changes in Greek and Roman politics. From these writers, the idea of a moderate middle class was appropriated by Italian Renaissance thinkers, notably Machiavelli.[2]

By the late eighteenth and early nineteenth centuries, the term middle class had become part of common parlance in Western Europe. Nineteenth-century political terminology identified the British "commons" and continental bourgeoisie with the idea of middle class.[3] With the passage of time, Western middle-class values, including those of the United States, became associated with a stable, hard-working, capital-saving _rentier_ type, who found respectability and success in belonging to the middle strata. This class, which in the West developed in large numbers, provided the social basis for the many moderate parties which aggregated the competing demands of the masses, namely farmers and laborers, and then adjusted their differences with the aristocracies. In the United States, differences between the lower, middle, and upper classes became somewhat blurred, until an overwhelming majority became emotionally if not economically a part of the middle class.[4]

With respect to Latin America, Johnson and other observers of his time hoped "implicitly" that a Latin American middle class would develop the same traits and play the same role associated with the middle classes in Western Europe and Anglo-America.[5] In all fairness to Johnson, it must be stated that his theses were wrapped in caution, as befitted a first-rate historian. Indeed, Johnson refused to use the term middle class in the Latin American case, noting that in other areas it had an economic connotation, and preferring instead labels like "middle sectors" and "middle groups."[6] Yet, he did view the Latin American "middle sectors" as the product of technological transformations which began in the late nineteenth-century and were widely felt by 1920.[7] These changes profoundly altered the static "middle groups" of the nineteenth century (the professionals, artists, artisans, bureaucrats, secular clergy, and junior army officers), adding dynamic new elements to the middle layers of twentieth-century Latin American society: factory-owners, managers, technicians, scientists, and in general commercial-industrial elements with vital stakes in the destiny of their nations.[8]

Although these new social elements lacked a common background, therefore not fulfilling "the central condition of a class,"[9] they did share a "common ground for joint political action."[10] Their cohesiveness was determined by six characteristics held in common. First, most of the "middle sectors" were urban. Second, having themselves received an education, they believed in the necessity for public education. Third, they were ardent supporters of industrialization. Fourth, they were intensely nationalistic. Fifth, they believed in a large government role in fostering economic development and social progress. Sixth, they formed a substantial sector of that public which was the social basis for the rise of social democratic parties.[11]

Although the "middle sectors" gained in influence, they represented a minority in virtually all Latin American nations, a condition which forced their parties to bid for popular support, namely from the "industrial proletariat."[12] In so doing, they demonstrated a moderate pragmatism which had been absent in Latin American political history. According to Johnson, "they possess the equipment for dealing with realities" and "they have accumulated in this century ...valuable lessons in the art of compromise." "The middle sectors," Johnson concluded, "have elevated to a new level the art of achieving some equilibrium by balancing a mass of political antagonisms. They have consequently become stabilizers and harmonizers and in the process have learned the dangers of dealing in absolute postulates."[13]

Thus it was that Johnson, writing at the high tide of reformism in Latin America, argued that a moderate middle class, reflecting basic social and economic interests, would pursue rational alliances with the masses and would mediate their demands against the oligarchy in the political arena at large. Unfortunately, Johnson neglected the psychology of the Latin American middle class, which was and is rooted in irrational and traditional drives. It is to this middle-class psychology which our analysis must now turn.

Whereas Johnson stressed the trend toward political change in Latin America, and the crucial role of the "middle sectors" in bringing it about, later writers have depicted the middle class as a barrier to reform and development. For example, Caludio Veliz has written: "In spite of its reputation for frequent and violent upheaval, perhaps the principal contemporary problem of Latin America is excessive stability."[14] Like so many other authors, Veliz blames a tradition-minded middle class for this condition. More recently, historian Frederick Pike has devoted an entire volume to an analysis of "the uncanny skill of the directing classes of Latin America in preserving the traditional social order against the multiple forces of change."[15] He, too, attributes this trend to a middle class which has become identified with the upper classes.[16]

Specialists from virtually all disciplines agree on one psychological characteristic of the Latin American middle class: that it lacks both cohesion and a sense of identity, and that its members tend to emulate and "ape" the traditional oligarchy.[17] Grant Hilliker, a State Department researcher, calls this emulation huachafo, and declares that the word sums up the basic differences between the Latin American and middle classes of other regions.[18] In writing of Chile, Pike declares: "Chile's urban middle sectors...have dedicated themselves to the defense of traditional, upper-class value judgments." In Chile, he continues, those who "ape" the oligarchy are called siúticos, and that nation's society abounds in such people.[19] This picture holds for most of Latin America, and it has roots in the history of social change in that region.

In formulating his historical hypothesis, Johnson attributed the expansion of the "middle sector" to "a transition from neo-feudal agriculture to semi-industrial capitalism."[20] He failed to realize that there was an important intermediate stage in the growth of the Latin American middle class: the development prior to World War I of an urban, commercial middle stratum which served an expanding oligarchy whose wealth was based on the export of primary products and foodstuffs. Hence, whereas in Western Europe there was a direct relationship between industrialization and the rise of middle-class reformism, this was not the case in Latin America. There, new parties were formed which did not as yet represent an industrial and manufacturing component. Between World War I and World War II, these new parties, backed by the masses and aided by junior army officers, came to power, thereby reversing an historical formula by which the attainment of economic power precedes that of political power.[21]

The rise of middle-class parties to temporary power did not, however, mean a successful alteration of traditional society in Latin America. In actuality, these parties did not seek to transform their societies, but yearned only for a piece of the "action," a share of political power and its perquisites.[22] Therefore, industrialization came to Latin America, not as a result of middle-class policy, but because of an "historical accident." This "accidental" industrial growth, caused by the economic isolation of Latin America during the Great Depression and World War II, did not prove conducive to the development of an "industrial culture" as a challenge to the "traditional, upper-class cultural complex." In contrast to Western Europe and the United States, an independent-minded, self-conscious, proud industrial middle class—determined to transform society in its own image—did not develop in Latin America. Instead, the Latin American middle class began to emulate the "cultural values" and "prestige symbols" of the traditional oligarchy. They enrolled their children in elite schools; bought land and horses; joined upper-class clubs; and imitated both the dress and speech of their so-called superiors. The middle class and the oligarchy thus "entered into an extraordinarily successful 'social contract,'" which dampened the reformist zeal of the middle class and precluded a challenge to the oligarchy.[23]

As the political scientist, Dankwart A. Rustow, has so ably written, the modernization of a society requires a certain degree of egalitarianism.[24] Both the pretensions of the Latin American middle class and the general psychological milieu of that region preclude such egalitarianism. As the anthropologist John P. Gillin has written, members of the Latin American middle class see "the universe, including human society, [as]...arrayed in a series of strata and the culture is still influenced by the value which he attaches to hierarchy..." "Under the weight of this tradition," Gillin continues, "it is not surprising that the typical middle-status individual sees most things in a scale ranging from 'lower' to 'higher'... In contrast with the United States' credo, Latin Americans do not believe that all men are born 'equal'... It is also obvious that, from the point of view of social rank, everyone is not equal."[25]

This Latin American-wide value attests to what Luis Mercier Vega has called the decline of the political power of the oligarchy and the victory of the "oligarchic spirit." The oligarchy may have lost much of its direct power, but its values have deeply permeated both the middle class and society-at-large. Mercier Vega described this development in telling terms, which merit quotation:

> No longer dominant, the oligarchy sees its spirit and manners copied by its social and political opponents. Disdain for manual work, contempt for the Indian, pride and conviction of belonging to an élite are no longer exclusive to the oligarchy. They are part of a heritage that is claimed or aspired to --with varying degrees of hypocrisy --by most of the groups who aim at political power even when they make a great show of their revolutionary principles, their admiration for the ancient Indian civilization, or their devotion to fulfilling the historic mission of the proletarian masses. In Mexico City or Lima one would be hard put to find a bank clerk or a student, no matter how

radical his politics, who would
degrade himself by carrying a par-
cel or do without large numbers of
servants--kept, of course, at an
Indian standard of living. Who-
ever succeeds in escaping from the
working class or peasantry immed-
iately dreams of entering the world
of many-faceted power, the world of
the oligarchic spirit.

Those who today aspire to power
project a type of society that
seems to have nothing in common
with the seigneurial domain where
the master, at the center of his
realm, was in complete control.
The slogans are increased producti-
vity, rationalization, the development of natural resources. But the
pyramidal form of the power structure of the new groupings, and the
attitudes of those at the top, are
strangely akin to those of the des-
pised and envied oligarchy.[26]

Middle-class disdain for the masses has deeply influenced the course of Latin American politics. Thus
it is that veteran Latin Americanist, Victor Alba,
speaks of the "schizophrenia" of the middle class--
"either it must arouse the submerged massed in order,
with them, to destroy the power of the oligarchy and
create a capitalist society; or it must make an effort,
from within the oligarchic society, to win control of
the government."[27] Fearful of the masses, the Latin
American middle class has chosen the latter course.
In terms of social revolution, the middle class faces
a dilemma described by anthropologist Charles Wagley:
"The middle class of Latin America helps create the
pre-conditions for revolution, but it really does not
want to live it through. To provide the same conditions of life for the mass of the people which the
middle class itself enjoys might well destroy its own
favored conditions."[28]

All of the foregoing positions on the tacit "social contract," as Veliz calls it, between the oligarchy
and middle class reach their climax in the work of
anthropologist Richard N. Adams. According to Adams,
social scientists accepted the concept of a new Latin

American middle class because it was a convenient, if invalid, concept for analyzing the recent history of that region. The usefulness of the concept of the middle class, he argues, has been greatly exaggerated. While it is possible to discern a growing middle-income sector in Latin America, the dual class structure has not changed. For the "new middle group is only an extension of the traditional upper class, both in terms of economic position and of basic values..."[29]

In a sense what has occurred in recent Latin American history is as old as civilization itself. As Gaetano Mosca pointed out as early as 1896, every civilization is subject to both democratic and aristocratic tendencies. "The democratic tendency--the tendency to replenish ruling classes from below--is constantly at work with greater or lesser intensity in all human societies." "But every time the democratic movement has triumphed," Mosca added, "we have invariably seen the aristocratic tendency come to life again through efforts of the very men who had fought it and sometimes had proclaimed its suppression."[30] According to Pike, these tendencies have existed in Latin America since the seventeenth century, as affluent members of the middle class were constantly absorbed by the oligarchy, a development which "contributed significantly to social stability and to the preservation of the two-culture society."[31] Hence, Adams the anthropologist and Pike the historian meet on the common ground of Mosca's historical insight--the absorption of an ambitious, tradition-minded middle class by the oligarchy in a "two-class" or even "two-culture" society. It is clear that Latin American studies have come full-circle since Johnson's hypothesis in 1958.

If then the middle class in Latin America is merely the tool or even the appendage of the traditional oligarchy, fusing with it from above and fearful of the masses below, must we junk the whole Johnson thesis? Not quite. A recent socio-psychological study of the South American middle class indicates an internal dichotomy between porperty-owning businessmen and salaried industrial and governmental managers. These sectors of the middle class differed in their "social cosmology." The businessmen believed that man's fate was determined not by the social system, but by the abilities of the individual. Poverty, they believed, was the outcome of deficient drive and ambition, and society must remedy it by improving the individual rather than by social welfare and trade unionism. Property-owning businessmen also were concerned with the dangers of egalitarianism, or the belief that society would improve if workers and peasants were better represented. On the other hand, the "new middle class," so dear to Johnson, the salaried managers and bureaucrats, believed the opposite--that social problems are the product of imperfections of the social system in Latin America, and these imperfections are due in part to "the lack of power of the poor."[32]

There is, then, a growing "new middle class" of salaried managers in Latin America which is socially-conscious and willing to compromise with the masses. But this is a lean reed upon which to support the Johnson hypothesis. For if Latin American history teaches anything, it is that economic success and upward mobility soon lead to the conservatism of those who made the climb. This lesson, so profoundly demonstrated by Mexico's ruling wheeler-dealer middle class, must now be discussed.

A key concept in this connection involves the recognition that the middle class in Latin America is the political class, delivering leadership and support to every part of the historical spectrum. This explains the variety of interpretations of the political role of the middle class since the publication of Johnson's optimistic views in 1958. For example, David T. Geithmann, sociologist, argues that, given a share of political power and social prestige, the Latin American middle class will enter into a right-wing "symbiotic" alliance with the oligarchy.[33] Still another sociologist, Luis Ratinoff, believes that when the Latin American middle class is in search of political power, it may prove progressive as it seeks to rally the masses to its support, a development which might have misled Johnson. However, once having achieved power, Ratinoff writes, the middle classes become defenders of the status quo.[34] In a unique interpretation, anthropologist Eric R. Wolf argues that some members of the middle class, torn between individuality and conformity to elitist modes of behavior, between autonomy and submission to oligarchical standards, may go radical and seek to tear down the entire "farcical" framework of middle-class values. Witness, for example, the case of Ernesto "Che" Guevara.[35] Finally, veteran Latin Americanist Irving Luis Horowitz argues that the Latin American middle class turns to the military out of fear that a democratic regime will inevitably yield power to the numerically superior masses.[36] This brings us to the last, and most complex facet of my study: the relationship of the Latin American middle class to the military.

According to Johnson, since 1930 the middle-class officers of the Latin American military establishments have turned increasingly from support of the oligarchy to support of the civilian middle class. This trend has been the result not merely of similar social origins, writes Johnson, but of a basic agreement on economic matters. Despite differences in political views, the military and the middle class "are in basic agreement on most major issues--industrialization, state capitalism, nationalism, and agrarian reform." They may disagree on such matters as the broadening of the political base or on the issue of internal communism, but their social and economic views are in harmony.[37]

Here again, Johnson, stressing rational social interests, has erred on the side of simplicity. As historian Robert A. Potash has written of the Argentine army, "to say that the majority of Army officers were of middle-class origin is only to say that they come from a heterogeneous social sector that was itself sharply divided in outlook."[38] In my studies of Argentine militarism, I have offered an hypothesis, which, while recognizing social forces, stresses the corporate-psychological interests of the military. It is true that, as Nun and Johnson have written, in the initial stages of professionalization, the newly opened officer corps of the Latin American armies strove to establish middle-class leadership in politics.[39] However, with the passage of time and the failures of the new middle-class parties, the armies began to develop values of their own which remained unsated by the reformist politicians. It was then that the armies, motivated by the corporate-psychological values of their officer corps, began to be torn between social order and modernization. In other words, the Latin American armies were and are both traditional and modern institutions, and they have been torn by this dichotomy in values. On the one hand, the traditionalist officer desired social order, hierarchy, a simple patriotism, a respect for national tradition, and a gentlemanly Catholicism. On the other hand, army officers are technocratic nationalists, who desire modern industry and a self-sufficient economy as the economic base of their war machine. To this day, the Latin

American armies have failed to bridge this dichotomy, a condition which explains why they veer from social order to modernization in coping with the challenges of Latin America's destiny.[40]

It must be stated, in conclusion, that Johnson made a great contribution to Latin American studies by his hypotheses on both the middle class and the military. As his study was born of the optimism of the 1950s, this paper undoubtedly reflects the pessimism of the 1970s. Much water has run under the bridge since the 1950s so that it would be easy to condemn Johnson's work with the magic of hindsight. Yet, even at this uncertain stage in Latin American history, one can hardly disagree with an increasingly typical judgment of the 1970s by sociologist David Chaplin: "The expectation that the growing middle class in Latin America's 'primate' capitals would at once lead the way to liberal reform and mediate the extremes of rich and poor to establish political stability is misplaced."[41]

Notes

1. Stanford, Cal.: Stanford University Press, 1958.

2. For a history of the idea of the middle class, see Arthur N. Holcombe, The Middle Classes in American Politics (New York: Russell and Russell, 1965), pp. 43-44.

3. Ibid., pp. 45-46.

4. Robert E. Scott, Mexican Government in Transition (Urbana, Ill.: University of Illinois Press, 1959), p. 78.

5. Eric R. Wolf and Edmund C. Hansen, The Human Condition in Latin America (New York: Oxford University Press, 1972), p. 193.

6. Johnson, Political Change in Latin America, pp. viii-ix.

7. Ibid., p. 1.

8. Ibid., pp. 1-2, 31-32.

9. Ibid., pp. 3-4.

10. Ibid., p. 4.

11. Ibid., p. 5.

12. Ibid., p. 1.

13. Ibid., pp. 193-194.

14. Claudio Veliz, "Introduction" to Claudio Veliz, ed., Obstacles to Change in Latin America (London: Oxford University Press, 1965), p. 1.

15. Frederick B. Pike, Spanish America, 1900-1970: Tradition and Social Innovation (New York: Norton, 1973), p. 9.

16. Ibid., pp. 31-32.

17. Karl M. Schmitt and David D. Burks, Evolution or Chaos: Dynamics of Latin American Government and Politics (New York: Praeger, 1963), p. 49; Grant Hilliker, The Politics of Reform in Peru: The Aprista and Other Mass Parties of Latin America (Baltimore: The Johns Hopkins Press, 1971), pp. 39-40; Charles Wagley, An Introduction to Brazil (New York: Columbia University Press, 1963), p. 126; Scott, Mexican Government in Transition, pp. 78-79; Gary MacEoin, No Peaceful Way: The Chilean Struggle for Dignity (New York: Sheed and Ward, 1974), pp. 8-9; Pike, Spanish America, pp. 31-32; Veliz, "Introduction," p. 7; Emilio Williams, Latin American Culture: An Anthropological Synthesis (New York: Harper and Row, 1975), p. 255.

18. Hilliker, The Politics of Reform in Peru, p. 40.

19. Frederick Pike, "Aspects of Class Relations in Chile, 1850-1960" in James Petras and M. Zeitlin, eds., Latin America: Reform or Revolution (Greenwich, Conn., 1968), p. 211.

20. Johnson, Political Change in Latin America, p. 2.

21. Veliz, "Introduction," p. 4.

22. José Nun, "The Middle-Class Military Coup Revisited" in Abraham F. Lowenthal, ed., Armies and Politics in Latin America (New York: Holmes and Meier, 1976), p. 58.

23. Veliz, "Introduction," p. 7.

24. Dankwart A. Rustow, A World of Nations: Problems of Political Modernization (Washington, D.C.: The Brookings Institution, 1967), pp. 80-81.

25. John P. Gillin, "Some Signposts for Policy" in Richard N. Adams, et al., Social Change in Latin America (New York: Vintage Books, 1960), pp. 34-35.

26. Luis Mercier Vega, Roads to Power in Latin America, Trans. Robert Rowland (New York: Praeger, 1969), p. 12.

27. Victor Alba, Nationalists Without Nations: The Oligarchy Versus the People in Latin America (New York: Praeger, 1968), p. 171.

28. Charles Wagley, "The Dilemma of the Latin American Middle Classes," Proceedings of the Academy of Political Science (Economic and Political Trends in Latin America), vol. XXXVII, No., 4 (May, 1964), p. 7.

29. Richard N. Adams, "Political Power and Social Structures" in Claudio Veliz, ed., The Politics of Conformity in Latin America (London: Oxford University Press, 1967), pp. 15-16.

30. Gaetano Mosca, The Ruling Class, Trans. Hannah D. Kahn (New York: McGraw-Hill, 1939), pp. 413, 417.

31. Pike, Spanish America, p. 32.

32. Arthur L. Stinchcombe, "Political Socialization in the South American Middle Class," Harvard Educational Review, vol. 38 (Summer, 1968), pp. 506-517.

33. David T. Geithman, "Middle Class Growth and Economic Development in Latin America," American Journal of Economics and Sociology, vol. 33, no. 1 (January, 1974), p. 50.

34. Luis Ratinoff, "The New Urban Groups: The Middle Classes" in Seymour Lipset and Aldo Solari, eds., Elites in Latin America (New York: Oxford University Press, 1962), pp. 61-93.

35. Wolf and Hansen, The Human Condition, pp. 199-200.

36. Irving Louis Horowitz, "The Military Elites," in Lipset and Solari, eds., Elites in Latin America, p. 152.

37. Johnson, Political Change in Latin America, pp. 13-14; John J. Johnson, The Military and Society in Latin America (Stanford, Cal.: Stanford University Press, 1964), p. 150.

38. Robert A. Potash, The Army and Politics in Argentina, 1928-1945: Yrigoyen to Perón (Stanford, Cal.: Standord University Press, 1969), p. 285.

39. Nun, "The Middle Class Military Coup Revisited," p. 58.

40. See Marvin Goldwert, "Dichotomies of Militarism in Argentina," Orbis, vol. X (Fall, 1966), pp. 930-939; Marvin Goldwert, "The Rise of Modern Militarism in Argentina," HAHR, vol. XLVIII, no. 2 (May, 1968), pp. 189-205; Marvin Goldwert, Democracy, Militarism, and Nationalism in Argentina, 1930-1966: An Interpretation (Austin, Tex.: The University of Texas Press, 1972), passim.

41. David Chaplin, "Blue-Collar Workers in Peru" in David Chaplin, ed., Peruvian Nationalism: A Corporatist Revolution (New Brunswick, New Jersey: Transaction Books, 1965), p. 209.

"About the Author"

Dr. Marvin Goldwert, Professor of History at the New York Institute of Technology, is a widely-published Latin American historian, and has also been trained in psychoanalysis. He received his B.A. from Brooklyn College, was awarded the M.A. and Ph.D. from The University of Texas, and served as a Research Fellow in the "Argentine Nationalism Project" at the University of Pennsylvania. His Master's Thesis on the colonial encomienda was translated and published in Peru by the Instituto Histórico del Perú. Dr. Goldwert is also the author of the following books: The Constabulary in the Dominican Republic and Nicaragua (University of Florida Press, 1962); Democracy, Militarism, and Nationalism in Argentina, 1930-1966: An Interpretation (The University of Texas Press, 1972); History as Neurosis: Paternalism and Machismo in Spanish America (University Press of America, 1980); and, The Suicide and Rebirth of Western Civilization: A Collage of Psychohistorical Analogies (University Press of America, 1981). His numerous articles, one of which was awarded Honorable Mention for the James Robertson Prize in 1968, have appeared in such journals as The Americas, Hispanic American Historical Review, and Orbis. In preparation for this volume, Dr. Goldwert studied psychoanalysis as a special student in the Psychoanalytic Center, New York City, from 1972 to 1975.